MY SUMMER
IN A
GARDEN

CHARLES DUDLEY WARNER

MY SUMMER IN A GARDEN

MICHAEL POLLAN
SERIES EDITOR

Introduction by Allan Gurganus

THE MODERN LIBRARY

NEW YORK

LIBRARY OF CONGRESS CATALOGING-IN-PUBLICATION DATA
Warner, Charles Dudley, 1829–1900.
My summer in a garden / Charles Dudley Warner.— Modern Library ed.
    p.   cm.
ISBN 0-375-75946-8
1. Gardening.   I. Title.
SB455. W29 2002
635—dc21   2001044974

Modern Library website address: www.modernlibrary.com

Printed in the United States of America

2   4   6   8   9   7   5   3

Introduction to the Modern Library Gardening Series

Michael Pollan

It took a woodchuck and a book to make me understand what's really at stake in the garden.

I'd come to gardening in the naïve belief it offered a fairly benign way to kill an afternoon, a refuge from the wider world, but even before the end of my first season I'd been forcibly relieved of my innocence. First came the rodent. A series of increasingly desperate measures to run a hungry woodchuck out of my vegetable patch escalated into a personal Vietnam (with me in the role of General Westmoreland, fully prepared to destroy the garden in order to save it), which promptly exploded the whole "garden-as-refuge" concept. The spectacle of my own rodenticidal rage suggested that more was involved in gardening than tending a few tomatoes and prettifying my yard. It put one into a relationship with nature that was anything but innocent.

But it wasn't until I cracked open Eleanor Perényi's *Green Thoughts,* a tart, smart, and beautifully written set of alphabetical essays (from "Annuals" to "Woman's Place") published in 1981, that I realized just how much was going on here, right under my nose. Perényi had found in the garden everything from sexual politics and class struggle to culinary fashion and, particularly relevant to my woodchuck problem, ecological insight. The garden, in other words, was better approached as an arena than a refuge, an idea I immediately seized on and have yet to let go of. Though I suspect neither party would especially appreciate the tribute, I can trace the discovery of my own vocation as a writer to the crossing, in 1984 or thereabouts, of that particular book with that particular rodent.

What Perényi had done was to introduce me to an unexpectedly rich, provocative, and frequently uproarious conversation that, metaphorically at least, takes place over the back fence that joins any two gardens in the world. Was there really such a thing as a green thumb? (Nonsense, said Perényi; why of course! countered Russell Page.) Was I within my rights to firebomb a woodchuck burrow? (Don't answer.) Must we concede the moral superiority of native species? And why is it magenta is so often maligned? (All too common, huffs Alice Morse Earle, before Louise Beebe Wilder leaps to its defense.) From book to book, across oceans and centuries, the horticultural backing-and-forthing unfolds with such urgency you'd be forgiven for thinking the fence of space and time were merely picket.

Right away I wanted in on the conversation, and, handed off from one writer to the next, soon made the acquaintance of a crowd of fine and fiercely opinionated talkers. There was Karel Čapek, a gimlet-eyed Czech who relished the human comedy he found in the garden, and Margery Fish, a gentle Englishwoman whose cottage garden in Somerset told the story of a marriage. Closer to home, there was Katharine White in Maine, reading her January harvest of seed catalogues as a species of literature; Charles Dudley Warner in Hartford, setting himself up as the Mark Twain of American horticulture; and Alice Morse Earle in Massachusetts bringing an almost Jamesian regard to the social swirl of her perennial border. (The peony, Earle wrote, "always looks like a well-dressed, well-shod, well-gloved girl of birth, breeding, and of equal good taste and good health; a girl who can swim and hike and play golf....")

Most of these essayists were moonlighting in the garden, which usually meant they were fired with the enthusiasm of the amateur and the liberty of the writer cultivating a piece of ground some distance from literature's main thoroughfares. Their voices could be by turns personal and prescriptive, diffi-dent and prickly, and, somehow, both self-deprecating and in-controvertible at the same time. Since these writers often came to the subject from elsewhere, they were particularly good at drawing unexpected lines of connection between what was going on in their gardens and the seemingly distant realms of politics, art, sex, class, even morality. I discovered that as soon as one got past the how-to volumes written by experts, and the il-lustrated coffee-table tomes of garden porn, the garden book-shelf brimmed with the sort of quirky, sui generis writing often produced by a good mind operating in a small space.

And so I read to garden, and gardened to read, counting my-self lucky for having stumbled on a sideline with such a lively and lasting literature. For what other pastime has spawned so many fine books? Only fly-fishing comes even close. (Numismat-ics? Woodworking? Macramé? Come on!) Which is probably no accident: for gardening, like angling, engages us with the natural world, as actors rather than passive spectators. Both put us smack on the frontier between nature and culture, which is always an interesting place for a writer to stand. And both literary traditions pose practical and philosophical questions about how we might better go about rhyming our desires with nature's ways, questions that only grow more urgent with time.

The books I've chosen for this series are the classics that form the backbone of this tradition. What you won't find on this particular shelf are reference works and strictly how-to books; there's plenty of how-to here, but the emphasis is more along the lines of how-to-think-about-it than how-to-do-it. Even the oldest among them will be contemporary in the best sense, offering a still-vibrant voice in the back-fence conversation gardeners have been conducting at least since the time of Pliny. I'm not sure whether or not we should be surprised by this, but a great many of the issues that engaged Pliny are the same ones that centuries later would engage Alexander Pope and Vita Sackville-West, Gertrude Jekyll and Eleanor Perényi, Charles Dudley Warner and Karel Čapek, and will no doubt engage gardeners centuries hence. I'm thinking of the power of plants to change us in mind and body, the gratuitous beauty of a flower, the moral lessons of the pest, the ancient language of landscape design, and the endlessly engrossing ways that cultivating a garden attaches a body to the earth.

Introduction

Sketch in Evergreen: Toward the Resurrection of Charles Dudley Warner

Allan Gurganus

> *The greatest delight which the fields and woods minister is the suggestion of an occult relation between man and the vegetable (world). I am not alone and unacknowledged. They nod to me, and I to them. The waving of the boughs in the storm, is new to me and old. It takes me by surprise, and yet is not unknown. Its effect is like that of a higher thought or a better emotion coming over me, when I deemed I was thinking justly or doing right.*
>
> —Ralph Waldo Emerson, "Nature"

> *A cauliflower? Just a cabbage with a college education.*
>
> —Mark Twain

I

Any gardener who has double-dug a patch of dirt for at least two seasons knows the shock: After three weeks' unpredicted rain, some plant—years dead and much regretted—simply reappears.

This can happen on the stickiest day of August. I mean that

rank moment when your weeds—beaten back all year, determined to set seed now that they feel frost dead-ahead—surge
upright like … well, weeds. And it's here we separate the gardeners from those who wish to prettify their yards. You must
simply fall onto your knees and weed by hand while making un-
attractive little sidelong grunts of pure exertion. And while you
squat here—slapping mosquitoes that drain your vital fluids like
the hummingbirds sipping from a nearby feeder just as red as
you are now—while you stoop there wondering if this unpaid
labor is ever worthwhile, you back into a miracle:

The very plant you saw endure its browning, endless, crispy
death two summers back, stands resurrected. It has tripled in
size. How often since have you blamed yourself for settling that
specimen into a spot so damp? You just didn't *know* it then. But
today, forgiveness, a comeback: The masterpiece has transmi-
grated five full feet. Taproot blindman's-buffing underground, it
has found precisely the dry soil that might've sustained it those
guilty seasons back. Bush-high, your old favorite intends to give
life a second chance and in your grateful company!

Of course, I've just described this banished durable little
book. Though tattered early versions still pass perennially from
hand to hand, Charles Dudley Warner's finest work has been out
of print a century and a quarter. And yet, with the help from
a few, thanks to its own banked vitality, here it stands afresh,
all glossy and spontaneously green again. Imagine the taproot
strength required for so stubborn a return.

You now hold the resurrected life-form of a sprig first planted
back in 1870!

———

During those prosperous cottage-garden years between the end
of the Civil War and the dawning of our newly passed American

Century, whenever the august *Harper's Weekly* needed to send forth some incognito fact-finding expedition, say, to describe social conditions in our formerly Confederate states still smoldering, *Harper's* naturally sought a team-leader renowned yet trusted. Some gentleman—sober, silvery, fair-minded—but twinkly-witty in his eminence. And Charles Dudley Warner was usually their man.

As emeritus editor of *The Hartford Courant,* as bosom-friend to those even better known, as editorialist and freelance expert on whatever national subject needed addressing next, Warner had already made himself a household name, at least in the houses of literate Americans.

True, he was never quite theatrical; not some professionally irreverent bulldog of honesty like his close friend Mark Twain. But Warner's spritely qualities far outstripped the hygienic-stuffed-shirt flavor that his triple-decker name still suggests. If not a force and freshet of universal philosophical inspiration like Emerson, alive and well across the Massachusetts line, Warner did espouse heartfelt, clarion liberal thinking. Still young, he had gone on record as an ardent opponent of slavery, a fervent champion of women's rights.

But, as I will attempt to show, the reason he is even half-remembered today has little to do with his statesmanlikeness, his erudite formality in the parlors and periodicals of Hartford/Boston. Warner's "public" persona—as reflected in his civic prose—was perhaps too filled with the gas and probity, the circular rhetorical excesses so perfectly reflected by those tufted itchy horsehair parlors of Queen Victoria's middle years. His "serious" essays—the screeds and opinings of a public man devoted to National Commonweal—can today sound as stultifying as they were certainly well-meant.

Warner is like many of us: Forced into an overly visible guardian's role, but best in his private utterances, surest within the holy precincts of his garden wall. It was in the company of his charming musician wife and illustrious friends, precisely when everyone was feeling most off-duty, only then did the Warner capable of today's Resurrection stir most readily to life. Here is the strange case of a Public Man whose Private Charm still renders him tentatively immortal. Our detective joy will be to trace the incandescent remnants of a fellow who became his best self only when most hidden.

When seated at the second-story desk that overlooked his own half acre's cultivation, only then did Warner relax into becoming the beloved "character" that his neighbors and countless godchildren adored. Safe here, eyeing homegrown greenery below, he finally unfastened his many collar studs and cufflinks. It was here Warner made his single and truest contribution. Here he became the man whose life force and joking company a hundred eulogies still describe. At his unofficial second-story writing station, with its garden view, Charles Dudley Warner helped invent—with this one slender book—a diverse and burgeoning modern genre that has long since forgot him.

———

But, before we turn to the happy reason that a footnote like Mr. C. D. Warner still deserves the rights and privileges of surging life, let us walk behind his latticed fence. Shall we stroll just here in back of the pretty stand of single hollyhocks and see what Time has left atop this gent's lush compost heap?

With his cufflinks in, with the celluloid collar-stays locked down tight, this is how the other Charles Dudley Warner wrote: I mean, when *watched*, when seated at his Doctor-Is-In official rolltop desk downstairs.

I quote a "Harper's Monthly" report called "The South Revisited." Published nearly a decade post-Appomattox, it chronicles his tour through the ruined Confederacy:

> In speaking again of the South in this Monthly, after an interval of about two years, and as before at the request of the editor, I shrink a good deal from the appearance of forwardness which a second paper may seem to give to observations which have the single purpose of contributing my mite toward making the present spirit of the Southern people, their progress in industries and in education, their aspirations, better known. On the other hand, I have no desire to escape the imputation of a warm interest in the South, and of a belief that its development and prosperity are essential to the greatness and glory of the nation.

ZZZZ. —Right?

In contrast, quick, let me throw open the street-side garden portal of Dudley Warner's present living book.

Compared to the above work's circularity, contrasted with its nearly comical Polonius-like pedantry, the tone of Warner's garden book feels so frontal, simple, trusting. Its tone seems simply human. It has no "desire to escape the imputation of."

I usually resent those friends who give away the ends of suspenseful movies: "Oh, you're going to the film where the guy's sexy girlfriend turns out to be a boy, that one?" But I surely won't be revealing too much of Warner's quotable book by citing certain merits of its first sentences.

Those lines enlist us by assuming our grace, our wit; those lines do not shrink from sounding opinionated, personal, rueful, knowing. They quickly risk the Theological—while remaining ever earthbound, embodied:

The love of dirt is among the earliest of passions, as it is the latest. Mudpies gratify one of our first and best instincts. So long as we are dirty, we are pure. Fondness for the ground comes back to a man after he has run the round of pleasure and business, eaten dirt, and sown wild-oats, drifted about the world, and taken the wind of all its moods. The love of digging in the ground (or of looking on while he pays another to dig) is as sure to come back to him, as he is sure, at last, to go under the ground, and stay there.

I count this a splendid wrought-iron garden gate, a see-through arabesque swinging onto the most promising of home-made vistas. I find Warner's starting-voice welcoming, fair, humble, funny, mortal, confiding, and—unlike this list—succinct.

I applaud the author's decision to make "Love" the subject of a gardening book's first sentence. I approve his choosing the, for 1870, surprisingly "low" form—not of poetical "earth," nor agriculture-school "soil"—but plain churlish kid-like "dirt."

So, even in the book's first sentence, we find the subject of humankind's greatest wish, its most soaring airy goal, already tied with the material—dust to dust—from which we, indigenous if complex lumps of it, derive.

Contrast this work's bold "hello" with the stuttering pinball-machine opening of Warner's "State-of-the-Confederacy" essay, a first sentence fully seventy-four words long. True, the work's next sentence drops to a mere thirty-seven. *My Summer in a Garden* begins with a fifteen-word sentence, followed by two breathed sentences of nine words apiece. If Warner's report on the South can charitably be called extremely "written," the prose of the present book seems instead both spoken and thought. It sounds inflected, casual, immediate. And therefore far more "felt." The tone's graceful use of the wry first person separates it from the presumptive quorum of "We."

Warner's garden book continually suggests, and with a poet's compression, the whole round of human life, the gallows joke of everyone's rigged mortality. All of that is faced in the first few lines then simply winked away.

"So long as we are dirty, we are pure." Given the lye-soap schema of nineteenth-century New England, from the mouth of a man whose name sounds like that of any village's highest-church Episcopal rector, Warner's Whitmanesque affection for healthy filth seems a radical idea, half-nasty. (Fact is, all gardeners can gauge the level of today's outdoors struggle by the darkness of their resulting bathwater. Was your day mud-brown, tea-amber, or mere amateur-sightseer's clear?) Warner's tone, his theme, the immense scope of his short work, are all set up, set out, in the very clay of these first four shapely sentences.

He at once places gardening where it usually falls within people's lives, at the late-middle, after their wild oats have been sown. He steps up to a lovely gust of nineteenth-century rhetoric (the crabgrass that would infest much of his later prose once this book helped make him widely known), "… drifted about the world, and taken the wind of all its moods."

You would not expect an austere Protestant newspaper editor to recall a word like "mudpies" (much less to recollect how to patty-cake make them). But Warner remembers. Throughout this work, he retains an open, marveling childlikeness. He remains boyish yet sage, as wise as excitable. This helps account for his book's great former popularity. (And this, I hope, will aid the work's second life in our Age far too secular and "adult," one far less willing than Warner's to see the God-likeness latent in a seed packet.)

Warner's open-eyed pleasure at the world helps explain why Hartford's citizens, young and old, professional and agrarian, held the author in such fond regard. While the brilliance of his table talk, the warming energy of his company are lost, written tributes still describe an immensely trusted person. As we follow him, page by page, month by month, along his garden rounds, Warner still leaves within these pages an unaccountable trail of happiness. It is a rare and all too transitory gift. Oscar Wilde, another genuinely virtuous man, once boasted, "I put my talent in my work, I save my Genius for my life."

Warner's books of "serious" essays, his trio of novels, today go doggedly unread. And yet, in the present work, we can still shudder at his retinal and sensual specificity. Here he left his purest sample of DNA, the humorous spur-of-the-moment presence burns through. As a teacher-guide and host, he is forever returning us to the wellspring image of Eden, first offered then rescinded. Warner's pagan affection for everything green, for all that's growing and gorgeous or edible, is forever enlarging itself via his church-bound New England taste of Overview.

Though this book has lain fallow for so long, its insights have all too often supplied (with no monetary benefit to Warner's heirs) the quips and pithy lessons favored by certain costly coffee-table gardening books, ones intent upon excellent color photographs and certifiable Inspiration.

My Summer in a Garden has withstood at least two of time's severest tests: its horticultural lore remains steadily applicable; and its spiritual lessons feel forever tonic, new, of use. Warner shows a wonderful gift for those polished epigrams that Wilde would bring to such berry-ripe perfection a few decades ahead.

Listen to our host running delightful theme and variation on a favorite vegetable after a particularly perfect growing season out back:

> Lettuce is like conversation; it must be fresh and crisp, so sparkling, that you scarcely notice the bitter in it. Lettuce, like most talkers, is, however, apt to run rapidly to seed. Blessed is that sport which comes to a head, and so remains, like a few people I know, growing more solid and satisfactory and tender at the same time, and whiter at the center, and crisp in their maturity. Lettuce, like conversation, requires a good deal of oil....

Concerning the author's own dew-spangled lettuce, no single epigram will *do*. He must endearingly plant many variants in a row, like those very heads of garden lettuce awaiting our own oiled and vinegared bowls.

As a companion, even in old age, Warner was much sought after by the children of his neighborhood. But kids too rarely write their memoirs. So again, the renowned rambunctious energy of the man is somewhat lost to us.

I can find but a single photograph of Charles Dudley Warner. Taken late in life, it shows a small, wiry gent, someone considering smiling while plainly wishing that this sitting—as in a dentist's chair—will soon end. Warner seems the opposite of his compeer, Mark Twain, who never met a camera he didn't like. Warner's white hair is shown cowlicked like a boy's; his preacher's black suit and clean linen is at least spared any encumbering necktie. But what really arrests us: the huge, mischievous, child-size brown eyes. They stare out as if to say, "What's up? What's most fun next?"

In the present book, we feel all the pressure of such patient playfulness. So much of good gardening involves a reckless willingness to shift this here, to put that over there—no, maybe not. As with life outside the garden, simply breaking even involves much poise and balance and is always labor intensive. If only you had moved that precious plant several years ago, it wouldn't have required the recent laborious resurrection. In chess, once you touch your rook or queen, you are obliged to permanently move it. Never so when we come to the earth. Reversals abound. They are required. Warner's book, for instance.

So much of successful Play involves an improvisational willingness to transform simple things into being briefly, yet intensely, something else. "Let's make the compost pile stand for the fort, see? And the Indians are maybe trying to capture it by coming at us upriver, meaning along the walk, and then these hoes had better be our spears and pikes and, before they get here, quick! it's our job to … hide."

Do you recall all this? Warner surely does. When he writes with such love of gardening, we feel an imaginative person easeful in a zone of his own invention. (Absent is the writing "pro" doing his best to enliven *Harper's* latest dreary preassigned topic.)

Instead, wander alongside, shoulder to shoulder, safe within the relaxed company of an affable fellow showing off such land of tilled abundance that he himself has hand-improved. Warner freely points out his mistakes and whatever notable beauty is in bloom TODAY ONLY. As with "live" theater, the very impermanence of gardening makes it so fiercely and instructively present-tense. Gardens die when gardeners do. Cultivation, like living, cannot be relegated to a hired staff, alas. Happily, certain books reverse this trend.

(My own favorite moment in my own backyard garden is the day's first patrol. While touring my plot of ground after a good night's sleep, the mug of coffee steaming in hand, before I've even brushed my teeth or dressed in anything better than an old robe whose hem is used to being dampened by the dew, I can show you at a glance how very much needs doing next, how very little I got right, how very much that costs me. And how much has changed overnight! Empires rise then fall in a single leafy whisper. One flower opens as another specimen, long happy here, simply fails to thrive this year. Which spiders have thrown up spans you must simply charge through? Such speed, set alongside steadying slowness, can make a single summer in your garden seem a perfect eternity.)

And, both our Virgil and Dante in this bower Paradiso, Warner offers us the ethical scope, the how-to knowledge, the comical upgrading elation required, to make the humble go epic. Here phenomenology gets hand-watered. Here the theosophist's worlds within worlds play themselves out amid the chess of lettuces. Here Transcendentalism is pruned then mulched.

How did that gray eminence C. D. Warner shift from a life so serious, solid, and informed—to the leisure sufficient to grow things, and then the wit to write of them with such speculative joy?

II

You already know by heart Charles Dudley Warner's most famous line. Typical, its being so often misattributed to his Hartford next-door neighbor Mark Twain:

Everybody talks about the weather but nobody ever DOES anything about it.

Aside from this undeniable witticism, the main reason Warner's name still bubbles up in ten or fifteen Internet entries: he coauthored *The Gilded Age.*

This novel, far from Twain's best, alternated chapters and characters with Warner's own signed contributions. The work is best recalled today for having lent its prophetic name to an incoming period of show-off wealth. The Astors and Vanderbilts—barons of industry, innocent only of income tax—threw dinner parties for guests seated, mid-parlor, atop live racehorses that diners surmounted via separate stair steps; the horses were well-attended arrears by broom-and-bucket-wielding servants wearing jockeys' racing silks. Meanwhile a few miles away, children of the poor were literally chained to dangerous looms for pennies a week. This Age was not, of course, solid Gold. That was merely applied, ornamental. A stick of the cheapest pine wood can be soaked in just such gilding. The strangely apt aftermath-pun falls on "guilt."

When Twain later dramatized this jointly written book, it became a profitable success on stage. Twain, like many great men of his period, was always making and losing fortunes; creditors would eventually drive him abroad for nearly a decade. But, anticipating literary history, in his stage version, Mark Twain untactfully deleted all those lines and figures that Warner had woven into the novel. Twain thereby reaped the full theatrical bounty himself. There's no sign that the deeply agreeable Warner ever once protested. He was probably in the garden.

—

Charles Dudley Warner was born in 1829 with a moniker that sounds the way toothpowder tastes—certainly good for you, but otherwise inedible. Maybe he courted the disaster of anonymity by using all three of his names? (I have a theory, bolstered by the fallen standings of two writers as gifted as William Dean Howells and Sarah Orne Jewett. Maybe to make your mark as a three-namer means you've more than tripled your risk of being lost in the mists of time? Surely Colette, that vivid tannic adamant immortal, had the right idea by bobbing her name. My esteemed prolific colleague, Joyce Carol Oates, will surely find this notion dubious.)

Though his name makes him sound like some Beacon Hill Brahmin, Charles Dudley Warner was actually born the son of a poor yeoman farmer in Plainfield, Massachusetts. His father, dying when the child was five, made a deathbed wish that young Charles be the first of his family sent to college. The boy must have already shown signs of the verbal acuity and genial temper that would later draw so many to him. His mother, taking her husband at his word, sold the farm to acquire tuition. She economized by moving in with women kin elsewhere. She at last managed to enroll her son in a boarding school, then sent him on to Hamilton College. Warner eventually took a law degree from Penn.

Like Twain, like so many of his day's "coming" self-made men, Warner worked an array of odd jobs. On the book jackets of our present age, novelists list their Ph.D's and honorary degrees. In the nineteenth century, that spot often boasted a roster of menial jobs manfully undertaken. Perhaps this knowledge and breadth of experience accounts for earlier fiction's larger sense of the world's workings, its rude muscular possibilities. Warner wrested from each position held a love of lore, a respect for the benefits of fine tools, a holy delight in all work accomplished.

He certainly read Emerson's exclamation: "Honest care and

pains yield to the operative. The law of nature is, 'Do the thing, and you shall have the power' … (Human effort) is one immense illustration of the perfect compensation of the universal."

———

As underpaid boys seeking their main chance, both Warner and Twain labored as typesetters; this helped each evolve into contributing newspaper articles, pieces that they themselves then had the task of arranging in lead type. This tedious job, so little changed since Gutenberg's day, would convince Twain to spend large portions of his own cash. He foresaw the press's next inevitable improvement; but his investments—in what would become off-set printing—came one generation too early to ever prove quite profitable.

A young man, Warner married well. After earning significant money selling prestigious real estate in Philadelphia, he moved to Hartford, buying part-interest in what became *The Hartford Courant*. Twain would try in 1873 to purchase a share in this newspaper. Warner declined his offer—underestimating the flashy fellow whose reputation was then but half-formed. Twain must've already looked like a fellow who might someday wear show-off ice-cream white suits year-round. And yet, neither man seems to have held this early impasse against the other. Twain simply invested in a Buffalo paper. But one year later, Warner had actually read the Missourian, was already learning from him. He urged him to reconsider, to come settle in Hartford. Of this reversal, Twain told his wife, "Revenge is wicked, and un-Christian and in every way unbecoming, but it is powerful sweet anyway." In 1871, the two writers became next-door neighbors, fast friends. The house Mark Twain built was as visually inventive as his own riverboat gambler appearance. Its foyer was patterned with what appeared mother-of-pearl inlay simulating American Indian motifs, likely laid out by Mr. L. Comfort Tiffany. (In fact, the mother-of-pearl was stenciled silver paint.) The home's brick facings were painted black and vermilion to look half-Venetian, half-Nevadan. Twain's mansion, the best-known survivor of what is comically called "the 1870s stick style," was the confident embodiment of his Age. Monticello is a home as personal as Twain's: The whole eighteenth century can be deduced from the place, its parlors, its scientific waystations, its extensive slavequarter. Similarly, the nineteenth century's cow-catcher energy, its opulent impenitent full-speed ahead can still be seen in Twain's rambling architectural invention.

The literary community gathered along Hartford's then-countrified Forest Street and became known as Nook Farm. (This name echoes Hawthorne's "Brook Farm," the communal experiment that ended so badly.) This neighborhood, chock-full of celebrities, warranted the equivalent to Hollywood maps of the homes of movie stars: stereopticon slides of Twain's home and Warner's were big sellers of the day. Warner's own house was a tasteful, commodious Queen Anne "cottage," far less insistently vernacular than his renowned neighbor's.

When his partner at the newspaper marched off with Federal troops to fight the Civil War, Warner—never gifted with a hearty constitution, and luckily nearsighted—assumed the editorship. We may guess that Warner was, during the worst and best days of the Civil War, becoming a better gardener (and writer) in that beloved little plot behind his home.

The period produced many gardening books, of course. But these tended toward technical manuals, works generous with proper Latin names of plants while holding back the poetry for italicized chapter headings (often listing Ophelia's incantation of wildflowers).

Since gardeners, in their gardens, are the most opinionated and boastful of persons, it might seem strange that books on the subject could have been so thoroughly given over to the driest news of husbandry and crop yields. Such conventional texts all lacked one leavening delight: the personable tone of a charming gardener eager to point out his failures as well as his triumphs. Missing: a voice subjective, qualified, admittedly flawed, and therefore humane.

Such a tone—rueful, self-knowing, and confessional—has often been sounded on the page by women. But garden writing by women is essentially a twentieth-century phenomenon. Twenty years after Warner's 1870 book, the Honorable Alicia Amherst published her definitive *History of Gardening in England*. It proved, alas, tastefully denuded of any narrative merely personal. Surely much or most gardening till then had been of the cottage variety and done by women. But the first major compendium by a woman quoted from and deferred to earlier male geniuses of large-scale gardening: Bacon, Bridgeman, Gilpin, Capability Brown, Repton. (Ms. Amherst banished her own most illustrious female contemporary, Gertrude Jekyll, into a footnote under the last photo in the book.)

———

Warner, trained as a journalist in how to be a cool if vivifying eyewitness, warmed this detachment with a style offhandedly folksy. And yet his voice—with its polished, shapely generalizing sentences—possesses a true, quiet authority. I would call it the prose equivalent of a clear conscience.

Surely gardening offered Charley Warner a no-pressure subject very welcome after Charles Dudley Warner's public assignments undertaken as duties to the nation. He wrote about horticulture not as simply a means to an end. Productive of more than produce, his own flowerbed seemed to offer him a porthole onto latent backyard transcendence. The seasons were a test, the soil required constant improving. And, as his soldierly contemporaries sent home their dramatic bulletins from the front, maybe this was Warner's news from *his*.

His joy in what was grown by and for civilians introduces a "Victory Garden" delight into the passage below. Here Warner lets his pride become first supercilious then finally adorable. He is, like some lively character in a good novel, usually quite willing on the page to make an utter fool of himself. Nothing—on or off the page—is ever more likable or ever more wise. In exchange, we recognize, forgive, and finally seek to defend this vain, half-bumbling but fully beguiling friend of ours. At the center of his each keen observation, we feel a developing "persona." Every reaction has some small emotional repercussion, every joy produces a fired shotgun's "kick" that might just leave a bruise. It is not simply easy to imagine Warner's good company; hearing the following, we are literally in it:

I know of nothing that makes one feel more complacent, in these July days, than to have his vegetables from his own garden. . . . The market-man shows me his peas and beets and tomatoes . . . "No, I thank you," I say carelessly: "I am raising my own this year." . . . I have never read of any Roman supper than seemed to me equal to a dinner of my own vegetables; when everything on the table is the product of my own labor, except the clams It is strange what a taste you suddenly have for things you never liked before. The squash has always been to me a dish of contempt; but I eat it now as if it were my best friend. I never cared for the beet or the bean; but I fancy now that I could eat them all, tops and all. . . . I think the squash is less squashy, and the beet has a deeper hue of rose, for my care of them.

The book you hold, like so many works concerning gardening, is a gathered bouquet of weekly hometown newspaper columns. (Since growing conditions are so specifically local, advice from a gardener six blocks away can prove particularly useful.) The brevity of the column form seems to bring forth the best in Warner. No seventy-four-word sentences here. Never a demand that this wry, funny, and modest man pose as The World Authority on anything—except perhaps the lettuces he's grown from seed.

Warner's first goal always seems to entertain. One need not be a gardener to still get most of his jokes. His humor has remained uncannily fresh. But, this being New England, and especially New England during a period of national cataclysm, the surface lightness of Warner's avuncular tone is always being pushed steepleward. He is forever urging us to seek whatever larger meanings can be gleaned from those blights and bonuses all gardeners are heir to.

Warner's weekly pieces were composed to be consumed in a single downward sweep of Hartford newsprint. If read aloud, they might each require eleven to fifteen minutes. In other words, they all run the length of sermons. And—like that hugely influential form ringing on throughout our national literature even now—each entry concocts its own chiming rise and fall. A stated problem leads to some ethical struggle resolving in a solution not unheartening. This shape can still be heard weekly, if often in tones and contexts less elegant, from your local pulpit.

How telling that the "discoverer" of these columns' power should have been the most famous preacher of the time. Henry Ward Beecher was visiting his sister, Warner's next-door neighbor, when the great man of the cloth chanced to peruse two consecutive weeks of an all-too-local gardening bulletin. Beecher was a figure and writer much esteemed; his endorsements were heeded then widely discussed. In our present age, place his station somewhere between a trusted retired U.S. president who hand-builds homes for the poor, an evangelical preacher always trotted out during national crises, and whatever leading Eastern light of self-help guided you toward a little inner peace most recently. The Reverend H. W. Beecher urged Warner to collect these weekly accounts into a book of their own. The preacher even offered to write its introduction, guaranteeing a far wider readership. The first edition proved the Reverend Mr. Beecher a man of his word:

> It is very plain ... that the author has long employed his eyes, his ears, and his understanding, in observing and considering the facts of Nature, and in weaving curious analogies. Being an editor of one of the oldest daily newspapers in New England, and obliged to fill its columns day after day (as the village mill is obliged to render every day so many sacks of flour or of meal to its hungry customers), it naturally occurred to him, "Why not write something which I myself, as well as my readers, shall enjoy? The market gives them facts enough; politics, lies enough; art, affectations enough; criminal news, horrors enough; fashion, more than enough of vanity upon vanity, and vexations of the purse. Why should they not have some of those wandering and joyous fancies which solace my hours?"
>
> The suggestion ripened into execution. Men and women read, and wanted more.... Now, truly, one may not learn from this little book either divinity or horticulture; but if he gets a pure happiness ... he will gain from our friend's garden what Adam lost in his, and what neither philosophy nor divinity has always been able to restore.

III

Charles Dudley Warner had, for any fairly well-known author of novels and nonfiction, the extremely mixed good fortune of living between one person who'd written *Uncle Tom's Cabin* and another who would soon write *Huckleberry Finn.* Thank God the preacher brother of the first at least saw fit to bind Warner's pages into this volume. But it cannot have been easy for any orginator of dreary sociological reports and daily local news to share communal wheelbarrows and fruit baskets with the two best-known writers of his time.

Abraham Lincoln, meeting Harriet Beecher Stowe, famously exclaimed, "So this is the little lady who started the great war!" Twain was not only the acerbic generous man quoted more often than any other living American, he had also contrived a national prose that was its most idiomatic and streamlined, the most electrically alive. Twain's was as different from most American writing of its day as Warner's formal man-of-affairs foghorn sounded utterly unlike the quickened flute obligatos of his garden writing.

If Warner learned Olympian subject matter from his neighbors in transcendent Concord, Massachusetts, he humanized those lessons via a fond jocularity practiced by the comic genius next door. It is often easier for the very famous to befriend persons utterly unknown. Better that than some big success condescending to a vastly smaller one. Writers, beings persons who make their living in private, employing enforced daily solitude, rarely actually enjoy the prolonged company of other writers, at least not for long. Once the first praise, the useful gossip ends, what else to say? "Do you use pen or pencil?"

That volatile thorny Twain trusted our serene herbaceous

Warner enough to share a byline, argues further this gentleman's brilliance at diplomacy and kindness. Warner proved a wizard at keeping himself in the good graces of others, even those never before known for their willingness to share the limelight.

Warner's slender book has left a deep if unacknowledged stamp on the way people write about their gardens and about nature in general. Though this might seem a modest attainment, though the genre could appear minor, some of the best stylists and thinkers of the century just passed were what we might call "nature writers." From Rachel Carson to Loren Eisely, from Edward Abbey to Annie Dillard and Ted Hoagland, through Michael Pollan and Nancy Goodwin, the list is long, loamy, immensely distinguished.

But Warner's originating humanity, his gift for mixing the Platonic with the plain, his bringing point-of-view to a genre once mired only in how-to, has gone unnoted. And, when a new high school had to be built on this once-famous block, when one home from among this literary trio's cluster had to be torn down, guess which fine Queen Anne manse went first? Both Twain's and Stowe's remain open as museums.

Harriet Beecher Stowe and Mark Twain appear to have depended upon Warner, adoring him. Twain's daughters called him "Uncle Charlie." They often took tea at the Warner place, always feeling welcome there. Friends admired Warner not simply for his garden, his neighborliness, but for an epigrammatic puckish charm. It still exists, the bittersweet green sap, at the center of this volume.

Influences that shaped his text aren't hard to guess. Apart from the structure of sermons, aside from the personable admissions more usual in letters written to close friends than in direct addresses toward serious and solemn readers, the urgent examples of the Transcendentalists stand evident on every page of this dewy work.

Thoreau's sole experiment in gardening, growing beans at Walden Pond, ended with self-disgust that he'd allowed one species to lord it over all others, hungry rabbits included. Who says weeds are "weeds," not simply tenacious and invasive wild-flowers? Like any mindful New Englander of his day, Warner knew his betters and read them all.

Hartford was then still surrounded by farmland, and Warner was a trusted local voice, a son of the farm. Emerson longed to be read by thoughtful farmers—maybe ones like Warner's own father who perished too young. Just how many men of the soil rushed out to buy Ralph Waldo's latest treatise on the soul has not been recorded.

But, at one remove, Warner applied Emersonian lessons of self-reliance, utter connection to nature, transparency to whatever theological reward the Daily offers. Warner sounds less doctrinaire, more localized than Dean Emerson as he strolls around a garden that becomes almost scarily visible to us as we read ourselves along its paths. Warner sounds a note more off-hand, more rawly autobiographical than Emerson's global Jovian overviews.

Warner's voice is forthrightly first person, more impenitently candid, far more the admitted concoction of a somewhat fictive persona. (He never, for instance, uses his wife's real name, Susan, in this work. Even the dedication is addressed to her in an invented moniker: Polly. This occasioned great disappointment for at least one voluble fan of the work who felt tricked and disappointed at the confiding author's seeming subterfuge.) Warner is usually funnier than Emerson. Though Emerson is never without a Mona Lisa smile, some warming merriment when noting certain overriding spiritual patterns. But Warner "cuts" the sacramental nectar from New England's high altar with some moonshine out of Mississippi-Missouri. He uses a wry, cranky humor, drifted over the back fence, to cross-pollinate and humanize his prose Emersonian. Mark Twain could steadily make garlands of what borscht belt comics would later call zingers:

> There is a marvelous difference in boats.... For a long time I was on one that was so slow we used to forget what year it was we left port. Ferries used to lose valuable trips because their passengers grew old and died, waiting for us to get by. She was dismally slow; still, we often had pretty exciting times racing with islands....

William Dean Howells praised Twain for *Life on the Mississippi,* the work quoted here: "It almost made the water in our ice-pitcher muddy as I read it." Mud again.

Warner shows a novelist's delight in the improbable, ungainly sacrifices all gardeners must make to Beauty. And to the mixed joy of letting others see it. One of my favorite chapters describes the strange sensation of finding a sitting U.S. president standing in his boots, up and patrolling Warner's cottage garden paths. U. S. Grant, as painted by Warner, is a rough but hilarious fellow. He had a good memory if a somewhat disappointing attitude toward what we would today call Chinese-Americans, not "Chinamen." Except for Grant's typical period racist quips, Warner's book might have been written last week. The language feels timeless, direct to the point of seduction. All the things that date Warner's *Harper's* essays on public topics, seem happily absent in his private views.

Warner, the gardener, is quick to admit his laziness, his vanity, his impatience with the job's inevitable discomforts.

I awake in the morning (and a thriving garden will wake a person up two hours before he ought to be out of bed), and think of the tomato-plants,—the leaves like fine lace-work, owing to black bugs that skip around, and can't be caught. Somebody ought to get up before the dew is off, (why don't the dew stay on till after a reasonable breakfast?) ... and sprinkle soot on the leaves. I wonder if it is I.

Hard to imagine Martha Stewart confronting this homely chore while admitting to such grumpy sloth. But Warner is not just a decorative gardener; his deeper interests run always to the ethical, the practicable. As we eavesdrop, he is steadily teaching himself; he is never out to "wow" us. Nor is he interested in shaming us with reports of his own diligence. Instead, he beguiles us, like a fiction writer, by allowing his very vices to seem eventual hard-won merits. His flaws first sound vain then silly, finally becoming familiar then representative. In the end, he is both a friend and a figure allegorical as some Bunyan pilgrim, hoe in hand.

—

Twain, avoiding bankruptcy and his mob of debtors, fled to Europe in 1891. Warner was desolated. Twain left his gardener specific instructions that Hartford's wandering bad boys should have free rein in gathering the bounty from his fruit and nut trees. Almost a decade passed. Twain, more famous and far richer, returned to Hartford again only in mid-October of 1900. And on October twentieth, just five days after Twain's reappearance next door, Warner died.

Given the nine-year lapse, considering the timing of Warner's expiring, surely he had been waiting for a last sight of his bristling, energetic friend? The funeral was said to have been one of the largest ever held in Hartford. (We speak of the town that would give the American arts both Katharine Hepburn and the poems of Wallace Stevens.) Despite Twain's wonderful riverboat of a house, after Warner's death, he chose to abandon Hartford forever.

Fourteen years past Warner's demise, the Reverend Joseph H. Twitchell, local Congregational minister and friend to all the Nook Farm writers, still recalled Warner. But even in the voice of this dear friend, we feel a certain devaluation of Warner's prose has already commenced. This contrasts with memories of the man himself, his longed-for sweetness, an ephemeral personality that has continued over time to gain in color and remembered value. Twitchell recounts:

> [Warner's] beloved shade haunts the places long gladdened by his presence, the echo of his voice seems to linger in kindly benediction, the unfailing delight yielded by the affluent felicities of the disclosure comes fondly back to memory; but the words in which they were clothed are mostly escaped and gone.

Except, of course, here. In this work we regain the delightful companion whose departure helped make Mark Twain the misanthrope of his later years. Here Warner remains a childlike force within the walled confines of his garden, his book, his garden book. No one ever became immortal for being kind to the neighbor kids, for serving as the most charming man anyone ever met, for being so thoroughly everybody's "Uncle Charlie." And yet, here in this one work, those are implied and can still be felt, enjoyed.

At the book's start, Charles Dudley Warner plants—with typical economy, harmony, and wit—this work's credo and his own.

The principal value of a private garden is not understood. It is not to give the possessor vegetables and fruit (that can be better and cheaper done by the market-gardeners), but to teach him patience and philosophy, and the higher virtues—hope deferred, and expectations blighted, leading directly to resignation, and sometimes to alienation. The garden thus becomes a moral agent, a test of character, as it was in the beginning.

———

ALLAN GURGANUS is the author of numerous works of fiction, including *Oldest Living Confederate Widow Tells All, White People, Plays Well with Others,* and most recently, *The Practical Heart: Four Novellas.* Among other honors, he has received the *Los Angeles Times* Book Prize, the Southern Book Prize, the National Magazine Prize, and the Sue Kaufman Prize from the American Academy of Arts and Letters. He lives and gardens in a small town in North Carolina.

INTRODUCER'S NOTE

Humbling how illusive Mr. Warner's trail has grown these last hundred and thirty years. Whenever I bumped into a guide who could lead me to some leaf-pile of three or four lovely facts, I felt such gratitude. (Maybe only a fiction writer, being charged with the invention of facts, can fully appreciate the genius of the literal.)

My friend Daisy Thorp initially recommended this work then lent me her own first edition. When the gifted Michael Pollan phoned, he had only to ask about "an unknown classic of garden writing" before I volunteered the title and promised to write its introduction. This would lead to much detective work I could not have imagined and, now that it's done, will never regret.

I found most helpful Garrett Condon's two-page Warner entry in his essay "Mark Twain in Hartford" (a work copyrighted in 1999 by Warner's former newspaper *The Hartford Courant*). Also useful, "www.booksites.com/stowe.shtml"—the Harriet Beecher Stowe website; I do like the sound of that.

Other works consulted: *The Gilded Age*, coauthored by Twain and Warner, Wendell Garrett's *Victorian America: Classical Romanticism to Gilded Opulence* and *The Illustrated Virago Book of Women Gardeners* by Deborah Kellaway. I've quoted Twain's *Old Times on the Mississippi*, which still contains, along with *Huck Finn*, his most muscular and naturally beautiful writing. I cite William Dean Howells's observations on the work as offered by Justin Kaplan in his introduction to the Perennial edition of *Great Short Works of Mark Twain*. I am indebted to Robert Richardson's dramatic definitive biographies *Emerson: The Mind on Fire* and *Henry Thoreau: A Life of the Mind*. I've offered excerpts from Ralph Waldo Emerson's essays "Nature," "Self-Reliance," and "English Traits."

Warner became most real to me via certain cigar-brown back issues (1850–1880) of *Harper's Weekly, The Knickerbocker,* and *The Atlantic Monthly*. These yielded the truest sense of Warner's former visibility. I hope that state will find resurrection via this, his lively bitter-green bud of a book. Long may it flourish afresh.

CONTENTS

By Way of Dedication

My dear Polly,—When a few of these papers had appeared in "The Courant," I was encouraged to continue them by hearing that they had at least one reader who read them with the serious mind from which alone profit is to be expected. It was a maiden lady, who, I am sure, was no more to blame for her singleness than for her age; and she looked to these honest sketches of experience for that aid which the professional agricultural papers could not give in the management of the little bit of garden which she called her own. She may have been my only disciple; and I confess that the thought of her yielding a simple faith to what a gainsaying world may have regarded with levity has contributed much to give an increased practical turn to my reports of what I know about gardening. The thought that I had misled a lady, whose age is not her only singularity, who looked to me for advice which should be not at all the fanciful product of the Garden of Gull, would give me great pain. I trust that her autumn is a peaceful one, and undisturbed by either the humorous or the satirical side of Nature.

You know that this attempt to tell the truth about one of the most fascinating occupations in the world has not been without its dangers. I have received anonymous letters. Some of them were murderously spelled; others were missives in such elegant phrase and dress, that danger was only to be apprehended in them by one skilled in the mysteries of mediæval poisoning, when death flew on the wings of a perfume. One lady, whose entreaty that I should pause had something of command in it, wrote that my strictures on "pusley" had so inflamed her husband's zeal, that, in her absence in the country, he had rooted up all her beds of portulaca (a sort of cousin of the fat weed), and utterly cast it out. It is, however, to be expected, that retributive justice would visit the innocent as well as the guilty of an offending family. This is only another proof of the wide sweep of moral forces. I suppose that it is as necessary in the vegetable world as it is elsewhere to avoid the appearance of evil.

In offering you the fruit of my garden, which has been gathered from week to week, without much reference to the progress of the crops or the drought, I desire to acknowledge an influence which has lent half the charm to my labor. If I were in a court of justice, or injustice, under oath, I should not like to say, that either in the wooing days of spring, or under the suns of the summer solstice, you had been, either with hoe, rake, or miniature spade, of the least use in the garden; but your suggestions have been invaluable, and, whenever used, have been paid for. Your horticultural inquiries have been of a nature to astonish the vegetable world, if it listened, and were a constant inspiration to research. There was almost nothing that you did not wish to know; and this, added to what I wished to know, made a boundless field for discovery. What might have become of the garden if your advice had been followed, a good Providence only knows; but I never worked there without a consciousness that you might at any moment come down the walk, under the grape-arbor, bestowing glances of approval, that were none the worse for not being critical; exercising a sort of superintendence that elevated gardening into a fine art; expressing a wonder that was as complimentary to me as it was to Nature; bringing an atmosphere which made the garden a region of romance, the soil of which was set apart for fruits native to climes unseen. It was this bright presence that filled the garden, as it did the summer, with light, and now leaves upon it that tender play of color and bloom which is called among the Alps the afterglow.

C. D. W.

Nook Farm, Hartford,
October, 1870

My Summer in a Garden

PRELIMINARY

The love of dirt is among the earliest of passions, as it is the latest. Mud-pies gratify one of our first and best instincts. So long as we are dirty, we are pure. Fondness for the ground comes back to a man after he has run the round of pleasure and business, eaten dirt, and sown wild-oats, drifted about the world, and taken the wind of all its moods. The love of digging in the ground (or of looking on while he pays another to dig) is as sure to come back to him, as he is sure, at last, to go under the ground, and stay there. To own a bit of ground, to scratch it with a hoe, to plant seeds, and watch their renewal of life,—this is the commonest delight of the race, the most satisfactory thing a man can do. When Cicero writes of the pleasures of old age, that of agriculture is chief among them: *"Venio nunc ad voluptates agricolarum, quibus ego incredibiliter delector: quæ nec ulla impediuntur senectute, et mihi ad sapientis vitam proxime videntur accedere."* (I am driven to Latin because New-York editors have exhausted the English language in the praising of spring, and especially of the month of May.)

Let us celebrate the soil. Most men toil that they may own a piece of it; they measure their success in life by their ability to buy it. It is alike the passion of the *parvenu* and the pride of the aristocrat. Broad acres are a patent of nobility; and no man but feels more of a man in the world if he have a bit of ground that he can call his own. However small it is on the surface, it is four thousand miles deep; and that is a very handsome property. And there is a great pleasure in working in the soil, apart from the ownership of it. The man who has planted a garden feels that he has done something for the good of the world. He belongs to the producers. It is a pleasure to eat of the fruit of one's toil, if it be nothing more than a head of lettuce or an ear of corn. One cultivates a lawn even with great satisfaction; for there is nothing more beautiful than grass and turf in our latitude. The tropics may have their delights; but they have not turf: and the world without turf is a dreary desert. The original garden of Eden could not have had such turf as one sees in England. The Teutonic races all love turf: they emigrate in the line of its growth.

To dig in the mellow soil—to dig moderately, for all pleasure should be taken sparingly—is a great thing. One gets strength out of the ground as often as one really touches it with a hoe. Antæus (this is a classical article) was no doubt an agriculturist; and such a prize-fighter as Hercules couldn't do any thing with him till he got him to lay down his spade, and quit the soil. It is not simply beets and potatoes and corn and string-beans that one raises in his well-hoed garden: it is the average of human life. There is life in the ground; it goes into the seeds; and it also, when it is stirred up, goes into the man who stirs it. The hot sun on his back as he bends to his shovel and hoe, or contemplatively rakes the warm and fragrant loam, is better than much medicine. The buds are coming out on the bushes round about; the blossoms of the fruit-trees begin to show; the blood is running up the grape-vines in streams; you can smell the wild-flowers on the near bank; and the birds are flying and glancing and singing everywhere. To the open kitchen-door comes the busy housewife to shake a white something, and stands a moment to look, quite transfixed by the delightful sights and sounds. Hoeing in the garden on a bright, soft May day, when you are not obliged to, is nearly equal to the delight of going trouting.

Blessed be agriculture! if one does not have too much of it. All literature is fragrant with it, in a gentlemanly way. At the foot of the charming olive-covered hills of Tivoli, Horace (not he of Chappaqua) had a sunny farm: it was in sight of Hadrian's villa, who did landscape-gardening on an extensive scale, and probably did not get half as much comfort out of it as Horace did from his more simply-tilled acres. We trust that Horace did a little hoeing and farming himself, and that his verse is not all fraudulent sentiment. In order to enjoy agriculture, you do not want too much of it, and you want to be poor enough to have a little inducement to work moderately yourself. Hoe while it is spring, and enjoy the best anticipations. It is not much matter if things do not turn out well.

What I Know About Gardening

First Week

Under this modest title, I purpose to write a series of papers, some of which will be like many papers of garden-seeds, with nothing vital in them, on the subject of gardening; holding that no man has any right to keep valuable knowledge to himself, and hoping that those who come after me, except tax-gatherers and that sort of person, will find profit in the perusal of my experience. As my knowledge is constantly increasing, there is likely to be no end to these papers. They will pursue no orderly system of agriculture or horticulture, but range from topic to topic, according to the weather and the progress of the weeds, which may drive me from one corner of the garden to the other.

The principal value of a private garden is not understood. It is not to give the possessor vegetables and fruit (that can be better and cheaper done by the market-gardeners), but to teach him patience and philosophy, and the higher virtues,—hope deferred, and expectations blighted, leading directly to resignation, and sometimes to alienation. The garden thus becomes a moral agent, a test of character, as it was in the beginning. I shall keep this central truth in mind in these articles. I mean to have a moral garden, if it is not a productive one,—one that shall teach, O my brothers! O my sisters! the great lessons of life.

The first pleasant thing about a garden in this latitude is, that you never know when to set it going. If you want any thing to come to maturity early, you must start it in a hot-house. If you put it out early, the chances are all in favor of getting it nipped with frost; for the thermometer will be 90° one day, and go below 32° the night of the day following. And, if you do not set out plants or sow seeds early, you fret continually; knowing that your vegetables will be late, and that, while Jones has early peas, you will be watching your slow-forming pods. This keeps you in a state of mind. When you have planted any thing early, you are doubtful whether to desire to see it above ground, or not. If a hot day comes, you long to see the young plants; but, when a cold north wind brings frost, you tremble lest the seeds have burst their bands. Your spring is passed in anxious doubts and fears, which are usually realized; and so a great moral discipline is worked out for you.

Now, there is my corn, two or three inches high this 18th of May, and apparently having no fear of a frost. I was hoeing it this morning for the first time,—it is not well usually to hoe corn until about the 18th of May,—when Polly came out to look at the Lima beans. She seemed to think the poles had come up beautifully. I thought they did look well: they are a fine set of poles, large and well grown, and stand straight. They were inexpensive too. The cheapness came about from my cutting them on another man's land, and he did not know it. I have not examined this transaction in the moral light of gardening; but I know people in this country take great liberties at the polls. Polly noticed that the beans had not themselves come up in any proper sense, but that the dirt had got off from them, leaving them uncovered. She thought it would be well to sprinkle a slight layer of dirt over them; and I, indulgently, consented. It occurred to me, when she had gone, that beans always come up that way,—wrong end first; and that what they wanted was light, and not dirt.

Observation: Woman always did, from the first, make a muss in a garden.

I inherited with my garden a large patch of raspberries. Splendid berry the raspberry, when the strawberry has gone. This patch has grown into such a defiant attitude, that you could not get within several feet of it. Its stalks were enormous in size, and cast out long, prickly arms in all directions; but the bushes were pretty much all dead. I have walked into them a good deal with a pruning-knife; but it is very much like fighting original sin. The variety is one that I can recommend. I think it is called Brinckley's Orange. It is exceedingly prolific, and has enormous stalks. The fruit is also said to be good; but that does not matter so much, as the plant does not often bear in this region. The stalks seem to be biennial institutions; and as they get about their growth one year, and bear the next year, and then die, and the winters here nearly always kill them, unless you take them into the house (which is inconvenient if you have a family of small children), it is very difficult to induce the plant to flower and fruit. This is the greatest objection there is to this sort of raspberry. I think of keeping these for discipline, and setting out some others, more hardy sorts, for fruit.

Second Week

Next to deciding when to start your garden, the most important matter is, what to put in it. It is difficult to decide what to order for dinner on a given day: how much more oppressive is it to order in a lump an endless vista of dinners, so to speak! For, unless your garden is a boundless prairie (and mine seems to me to be that when I hoe it on hot days), you must make a selection, from the great variety of vegetables, of those you will raise in it; and you feel rather bound to supply your own table from your own garden, and to eat only as you have sown.

I hold that no man has a right (whatever his sex, of course) to have a garden to his own selfish uses. He ought not to please himself, but every man to please his neighbor. I tried to have a garden that would give general moral satisfaction. It seemed to me that nobody could object to potatoes (a most useful vegetable); and I began to plant them freely. But there was a chorus of protest against them. "You don't want to take up your ground with potatoes," the neighbors said: "you can buy potatoes" (the very thing I wanted to avoid doing is buying things). "What you want is the perishable things that you cannot get fresh in the market."—"But what kind of perishable things?" A horticulturalist of eminence wanted me to sow lines of strawberries and raspberries right over where I had put my potatoes in drills. I had about five hundred strawberry-plants in another part of my garden; but this fruit-fanatic wanted me to turn my whole patch into vines and runners. I suppose I could raise strawberries enough for all my neighbors; and perhaps I ought to do it. I had a little space prepared for melons,—musk-melons,—which I showed to an experienced friend. "You are not going to waste your ground on musk-melons?" he asked. "They rarely ripen in this climate thoroughly, before frost." He had tried for years without luck. I resolved to not go into such a foolish experiment. But, the next day, another neighbor happened in. "Ah! I see you are going to have melons. My family would rather give up any thing else in the garden than musk-melons,—of the nutmeg variety. They are the most grateful things we have on the table." So there it was. There was no compromise: it was melons, or no melons, and somebody offended in any case. I half resolved to plant them a little late, so that they would, and they wouldn't. But I had the same difficulty about string-beans (which I detest), and squash (which I tolerate), and parsnips, and the whole round of green things.

I have pretty much come to the conclusion, that you have got to put your foot down in gardening. If I had actually taken counsel of my friends, I should not have had a thing growing in the garden to-day but weeds. And besides, while you are waiting, Nature does not wait. Her mind is made up. She knows just what she will raise; and she has an infinite variety of early and late.

The most humiliating thing to me about a garden is the lesson it teaches of the inferiority of man. Nature is prompt, decided, inexhaustible. She thrusts up her plants with a vigor and freedom that I admire; and, the more worthless the plant, the more rapid and splendid its growth. She is at it early and late, and all night; never tiring, nor showing the least sign of exhaustion.

"Eternal gardening is the price of liberty," is a motto that I should put over the gateway of my garden, if I had a gate. And yet it is not wholly true; for there is no liberty in gardening. The man who undertakes a garden is relentlessly pursued. He felicitates himself, that, when he gets it once planted, he will have a season of rest and of enjoyment in the sprouting and growing of his seeds. It is a green anticipation. He has planted a seed that will keep him awake nights; drive rest from his bones, and sleep from his pillow. Hardly is the garden planted, when he must begin to hoe it. The weeds have sprung up all over it in a night. They shine and wave in redundant life. The docks have almost gone to seed; and their roots go deeper than conscience. Talk about the London Docks!—the roots of these are like the sources of the Aryan race. And the weeds are not all. I awake in the morning (and a thriving garden will wake a person up two hours before he ought to be out of bed), and think of the tomato-plants,—the leaves like fine lace-work, owing to black bugs that skip around, and can't be caught. Somebody ought to get up before the dew is off, (why don't the dew stay on till after a reasonable breakfast?) and sprinkle soot on the leaves. I wonder if it is I. Soot is so much blacker than the bugs, that they are disgusted, and go away. You can't get up too early, if you have a garden. You must be early due yourself, if you get ahead of the bugs. I think, that, on the whole, it would be best to sit up all night, and sleep day-times. Things appear to go on in the night in the garden uncommonly. It would be less trouble to stay up than it is to get up so early.

I have been setting out some new raspberries, two sorts,— a silver and a gold color. How fine they will look on the table next year in a cut-glass dish, the cream being in a ditto pitcher! I set them four and five feet apart. I set my strawberries pretty well apart also. The reason is, to give room for the cows to run through when they break into the garden,—as they do some-times. A cow needs a broader track than a locomotive; and she generally makes one. I am sometimes astonished to see how big a space in a flower-bed her foot will cover. The raspberries are called Doolittle and Golden Cap. I don't like the name of the first variety, and, if they do much, shall change it to Silver Top. You never can tell what a thing named Doolittle will do. The one in the Senate changed color, and got sour. They ripen badly,— either mildew, or rot on the bush. They are apt to Johnsonize,— rot on the stem. I shall watch the Doolittles.

THIRD WEEK

I believe that I have found, if not original sin, at least vegetable total depravity in my garden; and it was there before I went into it. It is the bunch, or joint, or snake-grass,—whatever it is called. As I do not know the names of all the weeds and plants, I have to do as Adam did in his garden,—name things as I find them. This grass has a slender, beautiful stalk: and when you cut it down, or pull up a long root of it, you fancy it is got rid of; but, in a day or two, it will come up in the same spot in half a dozen vigorous blades. Cutting down and pulling up is what it thrives on. Extermination rather helps it. If you follow a slender white root, it will be found to run under the ground until it meets another slender white root; and you will soon unearth a network of them, with a knot somewhere, sending out dozens of sharp-pointed, healthy shoots, every joint prepared to be an independent life and plant. The only way to deal with it is to take one part hoe and two parts fingers, and carefully dig it out, not leaving a joint anywhere. It will take a little time, say all summer, to dig out thoroughly a small patch; but if you once dig it out, and keep it out, you will have no further trouble.

I have said it was total depravity. Here it is. If you attempt to pull up and root out any sin in you, which shows on the surface,—if it does not show, you do not care for it,—you may have noticed how it runs into an interior network of sins, and an ever-sprouting branch of them roots somewhere; and that you cannot pull out one without making a general internal disturbance, and rooting up your whole being. I suppose it is less trouble to quietly cut them off at the top,—say once a week, on Sunday, when you put on your religious clothes and face,—so that no one will see them, and not try to eradicate the network within.

Remark.—This moral vegetable figure is at the service of any clergyman who will have the manliness to come forward and help me at a day's hoeing on my potatoes. None but the orthodox need apply.

I, however, believe in the intellectual, if not the moral, qualities of vegetables, and especially weeds. There was a worthless vine that (or who) started up about midway between a grape-trellis and a row of bean-poles, some three feet from each, but a little nearer the trellis. When it came out of the ground, it looked around to see what it should do. The trellis was already occupied. The bean-pole was empty. There was evidently a little the best chance of light, air, and sole proprietorship on the pole. And the vine started for the pole, and began to climb it with determination. Here was as distinct an act of choice, of reason, as a boy exercises when he goes into a forest, and, looking about, decides which tree he will climb. And, besides, how did the vine know enough to travel in exactly the right direction, three feet, to find what it wanted? This is intellect. The weeds, on the other hand, have hateful moral qualities. To cut down a weed is, therefore, to do a moral action. I feel as if I were destroying sin. My hoe becomes an instrument of retributive justice. I am an apostle of Nature. This view of the matter lends a dignity to the art of hoeing which nothing else does, and lifts it into the region of ethics. Hoeing becomes, not a pastime, but a duty. And you get to regard it so, as the days and the weeds lengthen.

Observation.—Nevertheless, what a man needs in gardening is a cast-iron back, with a hinge in it. The hoe is an ingenious instrument, calculated to call out a great deal of strength at a great disadvantage.

The striped bug has come, the saddest of the year. He is a moral double-ender, iron-clad at that. He is unpleasant in two ways. He burrows in the ground so that you cannot find him, and he flies away so that you cannot catch him. He is rather handsome, as bugs go, but utterly dastardly, in that he gnaws the stem of the plant close to the ground, and ruins it without any apparent advantage to himself. I find him on the hills of cucumbers (perhaps it will be a cholera-year, and we shall not want any), the squashes (small loss), and the melons (which never ripen). The best way to deal with the striped bug is to sit down by the hills, and patiently watch for him. If you are spry, you can annoy him. This, however, takes time. It takes all day and part of the night. For he flyeth in darkness, and wasteth at noon-day. If you get up before the dew is off the plants,—it goes off very early,—you can sprinkle soot on the plant (soot is my panacea: if I can get the disease of a plant reduced to the necessity of soot, I am all right); and soot is unpleasant to the bug. But the best thing to do is to set a toad to catch the bugs. The toad at once establishes the most intimate relations with the bug. It is a pleasure to see such unity among the lower animals. The difficulty is to make the toad stay, and watch the hill. If you know your toad, it is all right. If you do not, you must build a tight fence round the plants, which the toad cannot jump over. This, however, introduces a new element. I find that I have a zoological garden on my hands. It is an unexpected result of my little enterprise, which never aspired to the completeness of the Paris "Jardin des Plantes."

FOURTH WEEK

Orthodoxy is at a low ebb. Only two clergymen accepted my offer to come and help hoe my potatoes for the privilege of using my vegetable total-depravity figure about the snake-grass, or quack-grass as some call it; and those two did not bring hoes. There seems to be a lack of disposition to hoe among our educated clergy. I am bound to say that these two, however, sat and watched my vigorous combats with the weeds, and talked most beautifully about the application of the snake-grass figure. As, for instance, when a fault or sin showed on the surface of a man, whether if you dug down, you would find that it ran back and into the original organic bunch of original sin within the man. The only other clergyman who came was from out of town,— a half Universalist, who said he wouldn't give twenty cents for my figure. He said that the snake-grass was not in my garden originally, that it sneaked in under the sod, and that it could be entirely rooted out with industry and patience. I asked the

Universalist-inclined man to take my hoe and try it; but he said he hadn't time, and went away.

But, *jubilate*, I have got my garden all hoed the first time! I feel as if I had put down the rebellion. Only there are guerillas left here and there, about the borders and in corners, unsubdued,— Forrest docks, and Quantrell grass, and Beauregard pig-weeds. This first hoeing is a gigantic task: it is your first trial of strength with the never-sleeping forces of Nature. Several times, in its progress, I was tempted to do as Adam did, who abandoned his garden on account of the weeds. (How much my mind seems to run upon Adam, as if there had been only two really moral gardens,—Adam's and mine!) The only drawback to my rejoicing over the finishing of the first hoeing is, that the garden now wants hoeing the second time. I suppose, if my garden were planted in a perfect circle, and I started round it with a hoe, I should never see an opportunity to rest. The fact is, that gardening is the old fable of perpetual labor; and I, for one, can never forgive Adam Sisyphus, or whoever it was, who let in the roots of discord. I had pictured myself sitting at eve, with my family, in the shade of twilight, contemplating a garden hoed. Alas! it is a dream not to be realized in this world.

My mind has been turned to the subject of fruit and shade trees in a garden. There are those who say that trees shade the garden too much, and interfere with the growth of the vegetables. There may be something in this: but when I go down the potato rows, the rays of the sun glancing upon my shining blade, the sweat pouring from my face, I should be grateful for shade. What is a garden for? The pleasure of man. I should take much more pleasure in a shady garden. Am I to be sacrificed, broiled, roasted, for the sake of the increased vigor of a few vegetables? The thing is perfectly absurd. If I were rich, I think I would have my garden covered with an awning, so that it would be comfortable to work in it. It might roll up and be removable, as the great awning of the Roman Coliseum was,—not like the Boston one, which went off in a high wind. Another very good way to do, and probably not so expensive as the awning, would be to have four persons of foreign birth carry a sort of canopy over you as you hoed. And there might be a person at each end of the row with some cool and refreshing drink. Agriculture is still in a very barbarous stage. I hope to live yet to see the day when I can do my gardening, as tragedy is done, to slow and soothing music, and attended by some of the comforts I have named. These things come so forcibly into my mind sometimes as I work, that perhaps, when a wandering breeze lifts my straw hat, or a bird lights on a near currant-bush, and shakes out a full-throated summer song, I almost expect to find the cooling drink and the hospitable entertainment at the end of the row. But I never do. There is nothing to be done but to turn round, and hoe back to the other end.

Speaking of those yellow squash-bugs, I think I disheartened them by covering the plants so deep with soot and wood-ashes that they could not find them; and I am in doubt if I shall ever see the plants again. But I have heard of another defence against the bugs. Put a fine wire-screen over each hill, which will keep out the bugs and admit the rain. I should say that these screens would not cost much more than the melons you would be likely to get from the vines if you bought them; but then think of the moral satisfaction of watching the bugs hovering over the screen, seeing, but unable to reach the tender plants within. That is worth paying for.

I left my own garden yesterday, and went over to where Polly was getting the weeds out of one of her flower-beds. She was working away at the bed with a little hoe. Whether women ought to have the ballot or not (and I have a decided opinion on that point, which I should here plainly give, did I not fear that it would injure my agricultural influence), I am compelled to say that this was rather helpless hoeing. It was patient, conscientious, even pathetic hoeing; but it was neither effective nor finished. When completed, the bed looked somewhat as if a hen had scratched it: there was that touching unevenness about it. I think no one could look at it and not be affected. To be sure, Polly smoothed it off with a rake, and asked me if it wasn't nice; and I said it was. It was not a favorable time for me to explain the difference between puttering hoeing, and the broad, free sweep of the instrument, which kills the weeds, spares the plants, and loosens the soil without leaving it in holes and hills. But, after all, as life is constituted, I think more of Polly's honest and anxious care of her plants than of the most finished gardening in the world.

Fifth Week

I left my garden for a week, just at the close of the dry spell. A season of rain immediately set in, and when I returned the transformation was wonderful. In one week, every vegetable had fairly jumped forward. The tomatoes which I left slender plants, eaten of bugs and debating whether they would go backward or forward, had become stout and lusty, with thick stems and dark leaves, and some of them had blossomed. The corn waved like that which grows so rank out of the French-English mixture at Waterloo. The squashes—I will not speak of the squashes. The most remarkable growth was the asparagus. There was not a spear above ground when I went away; and now it had sprung up, and gone to seed, and there were stalks higher than my head. I am entirely aware of the value of words, and of moral obligations. When I say that the asparagus had grown six feet in seven days, I expect and wish to be believed. I am a little particular about the statement; for, if there is any prize offered for asparagus at the next agricultural fair, I wish to compete,—speed to govern. What I claim is the fastest asparagus. As for eating purposes, I have seen better. A neighbor of mine, who looked in at the growth of the bed, said, "Well, he'd be ——:" but I told him there was no use of affirming now; he might keep his oath till I wanted it on the asparagus affidavit. In order to have this sort of asparagus, you want to manure heavily in the early spring, fork it in, and top-dress (that sounds technical) with a thick layer of chloride of sodium: if you cannot get that, common salt will do, and the neighbors will never notice whether it is the orthodox Na. Cl. 58.5, or not.

I scarcely dare trust myself to speak of the weeds. They grow as if the devil was in them. I know a lady, a member of the church, and a very good sort of woman, considering the subject condition of that class, who says that the weeds work on her to that extent, that, in going through her garden, she has the greatest difficulty in keeping the ten commandments in any thing like an unfractured condition. I asked her which one? but she said, all of them: one felt like breaking the whole lot. The sort of weed which I most hate (if I can be said to hate any thing which grows in my own garden) is the "pusley," a fat, ground-clinging, spreading, greasy thing, and the most propagatious (it is not my fault if the word is not in the dictionary) plant I know. I saw a Chinaman, who came over with a returned missionary, and pretended to be converted, boil a lot of it in a pot, stir in eggs, and mix and eat it with relish,—"Me likee he." It will be a good thing to keep the Chinamen on when they come to do our gardening. I only fear they will cultivate it at the expense of the strawberries and melons. Who can say that other weeds, which we despise, may not be the favorite food of some remote people or tribe. We ought to abate our conceit. It is possible that we destroy in our gardens that which is really of most value in some other place. Perhaps, in like manner, our faults and vices are virtues in some remote planet. I cannot see, however, that this thought is of the slightest value to us here, any more than weeds are.

There is another subject which is forced upon my notice. I like neighbors, and I like chickens; but I do not think they ought to be united near a garden. Neighbors' hens in your garden are an annoyance. Even if they did not scratch up the corn, and peck the strawberries, and eat the tomatoes, it is not pleasant to see them straddling about in their jerky, high-stepping, speculative manner, picking inquisitively here and there. It is of no use to tell the neighbor that his hens eat your tomatoes: it makes no impression on him, for the tomatoes are not his. The best way is to casually remark to him that he has a fine lot of chickens, pretty well grown, and that you like spring chickens broiled. He will take them away at once. The neighbors' small children are also out of place in your garden, in strawberry and currant time. I hope I appreciate the value of children. We should soon come to nothing without them, though the Shakers have the best gardens in the world. Without them the common school would languish. But the problem is, what to do with them in a garden. For they are not good to eat, and there is a law against making away with them. The law is not very well enforced, it is true; for people do thin them out with constant dosing, paregoric, and soothing-sirups, and scanty clothing. But I, for one, feel that it would not be right, aside from the law, to take the life, even of the smallest child, for the sake of a little fruit, more or less, in the garden. I may be wrong; but these are my sentiments, and I am not ashamed of them. When we come, as Bryant says in his "Iliad," to leave the circus of this life, and join that innumerable caravan which moves, it will be some satisfaction to us, that we have never, in the way of gardening, disposed of even the humblest child unnecessarily. My plan would be to put them into Sunday schools more thoroughly, and to give the Sunday schools an agricultural turn; teaching the children the sacredness of neighbors' vegetables. I think that our Sunday schools do not sufficiently impress upon children the danger, from snakes and otherwise, of going into the neighbors' gardens.

Sixth Week

Somebody has sent me a new sort of hoe, with the wish that I should speak favorably of it, if I can consistently. I willingly do so, but with the understanding that I am to be at liberty to speak just as courteously of any other hoe which I may receive. If I understand religious morals, this is the position of the religious press with regard to bitters and wringing-machines. In some cases, the responsibility of such a recommendation is shifted upon the wife of the editor or clergyman. Polly says she is entirely willing to make a certificate, accompanied with an affidavit, with regard to this hoe; but her habit of sitting about the garden-walk, on an inverted flower-pot, while I hoe, somewhat destroys the practical value of her testimony.

As to this hoe, I do not mind saying that it has changed my view of the desirableness and value of human life. It has, in fact, made life a holiday to me. It is made on the principle that man is an upright, sensible, reasonable being, and not a grovelling wretch. It does away with the necessity of the hinge in the back. The handle is seven and a half feet long. There are two narrow blades, sharp on both edges, which come together at an obtuse angle in front; and as you walk along with this hoe before you, pushing and pulling with a gentle motion, the weeds fall at every thrust and withdrawal, and the slaughter is immediate and wide-spread. When I got this hoe, I was troubled with sleepless mornings, pains in the back, kleptomania with regard to new weeders; when I went into my garden, I was always sure to see something. In this disordered state of mind and body, I got this hoe. The morning after a day of using it, I slept perfectly and late. I regained my respect for the eighth commandment. After two doses of the hoe in the garden, the weeds entirely disappeared. Trying it a third morning, I was obliged to throw it over the fence in order to save from destruction the green things that ought to grow in the garden. Of course, this is figurative language. What I mean is, that the fascination of using this hoe is such, that you are sorely tempted to employ it upon your vegetables, after the weeds are laid low, and must hastily withdraw it, to avoid unpleasant results. I make this explanation, because I intend to put nothing into these agricultural papers that will not bear the strictest scientific investigation; nothing that the youngest child cannot understand and cry for; nothing that the oldest and wisest men will not need to study with care.

I need not add, that the care of a garden with this hoe becomes the merest pastime. I would not be without one for a single night. The only danger is, that you may rather make an idol of the hoe, and somewhat neglect your garden in explaining it, and fooling about with it. I almost think, that, with one of these in the hands of an ordinary day-laborer, you might see at night where he had been working.

Let us have peas. I have been a zealous advocate of the birds. I have rejoiced in their multiplication. I have endured their concerts at four o'clock in the morning without a murmur. Let them come, I said, and eat the worms, in order that we, later, may enjoy the foliage and the fruits of the earth. We have a cat, a magnificent animal, of the sex which votes (but not a pole-cat),—so large and powerful, that, if he were in the army, he would be called Long Tom. He is a cat of fine disposition, the most irreproachable morals I ever saw thrown away in a cat, and a splendid hunter. He spends his nights, not in social dissipation, but in gathering in rats, mice, flying-squirrels, and also birds. When he first brought me a bird, I told him that it was wrong, and tried to convince him, while he was eating it, that he was doing wrong; for he is a reasonable cat, and understands pretty much every thing except the binomial theorem and the time down the cycloidal arc. But with no effect. The killing of birds went on to my great regret and shame.

The other day, I went to my garden to get a mess of peas. I had seen, the day before, that they were just ready to pick. How I had lined the ground, planted, hoed, bushed them! The bushes were very fine,—seven feet high, and of good wood. How I had delighted in the growing, the blowing, the podding! What a touching thought it was that they had all podded for me! When I went to pick them, I found the pods all split open, and the peas gone. The dear little birds, who are so fond of the strawberries, had eaten them all. Perhaps there were left as many as I planted: I did not count them. I made a rapid estimate of the cost of the seed, the interest of the ground, the price of labor, the value of the bushes, the anxiety of weeks of watchfulness. I looked about me on the face of Nature. The wind blew from the south so soft and treacherous! A thrush sang in the woods so deceitfully! All Nature seemed fair. But who was to give me back my peas? The fowls of the air have peas; but what has man?

I went into the house. I called Calvin. (That is the name of our cat, given him on account of his gravity, morality, and uprightness. We never familiarly call him John.) I petted Calvin. I lavished upon him an enthusiastic fondness. I told him that he had no fault; that the one action that I had called a vice was an heroic exhibition of regard for my interests. I bade him go and do likewise continually. I now saw how much better instinct is than mere unguided reason. Calvin knew. If he had put his opinion into English (instead of his native catalogue), it would have been: "You need not teach your grandmother to suck eggs." It was only the round of Nature. The worms eat a noxious something in the ground. The birds eat the worms. Calvin eats the birds. We eat—no, we do not eat Calvin. There the chain stops. When you ascend the scale of being, and come to an animal that is, like ourselves, inedible, you have arrived at a result where you can rest. Let us respect the cat. He completes an edible chain.

I have little heart to discuss methods of raising peas. It occurs to me that I can have an iron pea-bush, a sort of trellis, through which I could discharge electricity at frequent intervals, and electrify the birds to death when they alight; for they stand upon my beautiful brush in order to pick out the peas. An apparatus of this kind, with an operator, would cost, however, about as much as the peas. A neighbor suggests, that I might put up a scarecrow near the vines, which would keep the birds away. I am doubtful about it: the birds are too much accustomed to seeing a person in poor clothes in the garden to care much for that. Another neighbor suggests, that the birds do not open the pods; that a sort of blast, apt to come after rain, splits the pods, and the birds then eat the peas. It may be so. There seems to be complete unity of action between the blast and the birds. But good neighbors, kind friends, I desire that you will not increase, by talk, a disappointment which you cannot assuage.

Seventh Week

A garden is an awful responsibility. You never know what you may be aiding to grow in it. I heard a sermon, not long ago, in which the preacher said that the Christian, at the moment of his becoming one, was as perfect a Christian as he would be if he grew to be an archangel; that is, that he would not change thereafter at all, but only develop. I do not know whether this is good theology, or not; and I hesitate to support it by an illustration from my garden, especially as I do not want to run the risk of propagating error, and I do not care to give away these theological comparisons to clergymen who make me so little return in the way of labor. But I find, in dissecting a pea-blossom, that hidden in the centre of it is a perfect miniature pea-pod, with the peas all in it,—as perfect a pea-pod as it will ever be; only it is as tiny as a chatelaine ornament. Maize and some other things show the same precocity. This confirmation of the theologic theory is startling, and sets me meditating upon the moral possibilities of my garden. I may find in it yet the cosmic egg.

And, speaking of moral things, I am half determined to petition the Œcumenical Council to issue a bull of excommunication against "pusley." Of all the forms which "error" has taken in this world, I think that is about the worst. In the middle ages, the monks in St. Bernard's ascetic community at Clairvaux excommunicated a vineyard which a less rigid monk had planted near, so that it bore nothing. In 1120, a bishop of Laon excommunicated the caterpillars in his diocese; and, the following year, St. Bernard excommunicated the flies in the Monastery of Foigny; and in 1510 the ecclesiastical court pronounced the dread sentence against the rats of Autun, Macon, and Lyons. These examples are sufficient precedents. It will be well for the council, however, not to publish the bull either just before or just after a rain; for nothing can kill this pestilent heresy when the ground is wet.

It is the time of festivals. Polly says we ought to have one,—a strawberry-festival. She says they are perfectly delightful: it is so nice to get people together!—this hot weather. They create such a good feeling! I myself am very fond of festivals. I always go,—when I can consistently. Besides the strawberries, there are ice-creams and cake and lemonade, and that sort of thing; and one always feels so well the next day after such a diet! But as social re-unions, if there are good things to eat, nothing can be pleasanter; and they are very profitable, if you have a good object. I agreed that we ought to have a festival; but I did not know what object to devote it to. We are not in need of an organ, not of any pulpit-cushions. I do not know as they use pulpit-cushions now as much as they used to, when preachers had to have something soft to pound, so that they would not hurt their fists. I suggested pocket-handkerchiefs, and flannels for next winter. But Polly says that will not do at all. You must have some charitable object,— something that appeals to a vast sense of something; something that it will be right to get up lotteries and that sort of thing for. I suggest a festival for the benefit of my garden; and this seems feasible. In order to make every thing pass off pleasantly, invited guests will bring or send their own strawberries and cream, which I shall be happy to sell to them at a slight advance. There are a great many improvements which the garden needs; among them a sounding-board, so that the neighbors' children can hear when I tell them to get a little farther off from the currant-bushes. I should also like a selection from the ten command-ments, in big letters, posted up conspicuously, and a few traps, that will detain, but not maim, for the benefit of those who can-not read. But what is most important is, that the ladies should crochet nets to cover over the strawberries. A good-sized, well-managed festival ought to produce nets enough to cover my entire beds; and I can think of no other method of preserving the berries from the birds next year. I wonder how many straw-berries it would need for a festival, and whether they would cost more than the nets.

I am more and more impressed, as the summer goes on, with the inequality of man's fight with Nature; especially in a civi-lized state. In savagery, it does not so much matter; for one does not take a square hold, and put out his strength, but rather ac-commodates himself to the situation, and takes what he can get, without raising any dust, or putting himself into everlasting op-position. But the minute he begins to clear a spot larger than he needs to sleep in for a night, and to try to have his own way in the least, Nature is at once up, and vigilant, and contests him at every step with all her ingenuity and unwearied vigor. This talk of subduing Nature is pretty much nonsense. I do not intend to surrender in the midst of the summer campaign, yet I cannot but think how much more peaceful my relations would now be with the primal forces, if I had let Nature make the garden according to her own notion. (This is written with the thermometer at ninety degrees, and the weeds starting up with a freshness and vigor, as if they had just thought of it for the first time, and had not been cut down and dragged out every other day since the snow went off.)

We have got down the forests, and exterminated savage beasts; but Nature is no more subdued than before: she only changes her tactics,—uses smaller guns, so to speak. She re-enforces herself with a variety of bugs, worms, and vermin, and weeds, unknown to the savage state, in order to make war upon the things of our planting; and calls in the fowls of the air, just as we think the battle is won, to snatch away the booty. When one gets almost weary of the struggle, she is as fresh as at the beginning,—just, in fact, ready for the fray. I, for my part, begin to appreciate the value of frost and snow; for they give the husbandman a little peace, and enable him, for a season, to contemplate his incessant foe subdued. I do not wonder that the tropical people, where Nature never goes to sleep, give it up, and sit in lazy acquiescence.

Here I have been working all the season to make a piece of lawn. It had to be graded and sowed and rolled; and I have been shaving it like a barber. When it was soft, every thing had a tendency to go on to it,—cows, and especially wandering hackmen. Hackmen (who are a product of civilization) know a lawn when they see it. They rather have a fancy for it, and always try to drive so as to cut the sharp borders of it, and leave the marks of their wheels in deep ruts of cut-up, ruined turf. The other morning, I had just been running the mower over the lawn, and stood regarding its smoothness, when I noticed one, two, three puffs of fresh earth in it; and, hastening thither, I found that the mole had arrived to complete the work of the hackmen. In a half-hour, he had rooted up the ground like a pig. I found his run-ways. I waited for him with a spade. He did not appear; but, the next time I passed by, he had ridged the ground in all directions,—a smooth, beautiful animal, with fur like silk, if you could only catch him. He appears to enjoy the lawn as much as the hackmen did. He does not care how smooth it is. He is constantly mining, and ridging it up. I am not sure but he could be counter-mined. I have half a mind to put powder in here and there, and blow the whole thing into the air. Some folks set traps for the mole; but my moles never seem to go twice in the same place. I am not sure but it would bother them to sow the lawn with interlacing snake-grass (the botanical name of which, somebody writes me, is devil-grass: the first time I have heard that the Devil has a botanical name), which would worry them, if it is as difficult for them to get through it as it is for me.

I do not speak of this mole in any tone of complaint. He is only a part of the untiring resources which Nature brings against the humble gardener. I desire to write nothing against him which I should wish to recall at the last,—nothing foreign to the spirit of that beautiful saying of the dying boy, "He had no copy-book, which, dying, he was sorry he had blotted."

EIGHTH WEEK

My garden has been visited by a High Official Person. President G—nt was here just before the Fourth, getting his mind quiet for that event by a few days of retirement, staying with a friend at the head of our street; and I asked him if he wouldn't like to come down our way Sunday afternoon, and take a plain, simple look at my garden, eat a little lemon ice-cream and jelly-cake, and drink a glass of native lager-bier. I thought of putting up over my gate, "Welcome to the Nation's Gardener;" but I hate nonsense, and didn't do it. I, however, hoed diligently on Saturday: what weeds I couldn't remove I buried, so that every thing would look all right. The borders of my drive were trimmed with scissors; and every thing that could offend the Eye of the Great was hustled out of the way.

In relating this interview, it must be distinctly understood that I am not responsible for any thing that the president said; nor is he, either. He is not a great speaker; but whatever he says has an esoteric and an exoteric meaning; and some of his remarks about my vegetables went very deep. I said nothing to him whatever about politics, at which he seemed a good deal surprised: he said it was the first garden he had ever been in, with a man, when the talk was not of appointments. I told him that this was purely vegetable; after which he seemed more at his ease, and, in fact, delighted with every thing he saw. He was much interested in my strawberry-beds, asked what varieties I had, and requested me to send him some seed. He said the patent-office seed was as difficult to raise as an appropriation for the St. Domingo business. The playful bean seemed also to please him; and he said he had never seen such impressive corn and potatoes at this time of year; that it was to him an unexpected pleasure, and one of the choicest memories that he should take away with him of his visit to New England.

N.B.—That corn and those potatoes which Gen. Gr—nt looked at, I will sell for seed, at five dollars an ear, and one dollar a potato. Office-seekers need not apply.

Knowing the president's great desire for peas, I kept him from that part of the garden where the vines grow. But they could not be concealed. Those who say that the president is not a man easily moved are knaves or fools. When he saw my pea-pods, ravaged by the birds, he burst into tears. A man of war, he knows the value of peas. I told him they were an excellent sort, "The Champion of England." As quick as a flash, he said,—

"Why don't you call them 'The Reverdy Johnson' "?

It was a very clever *bon-mot*; but I changed the subject.

The sight of my squashes, with stalks as big as speaking-trumpets, restored the president to his usual spirits. He said the summer squash was the most ludicrous vegetable he knew. It was nearly all leaf and blow, with only a sickly, crook-necked fruit after a mighty fuss. It reminded him of the member of Congress from ———; but I hastened to change the subject.

As we walked along, the keen eye of the president rested upon some handsome sprays of "pusley," which must have grown up since Saturday night. It was most fortunate; for it led his excellency to speak of the Chinese problem. He said he had been struck with one coupling of the Chinese and "pusley" in one of my agricultural papers; and it had a significance more far-reaching than I had probably supposed. He had made the Chinese problem a special study. He said that I was right in saying that "pusley" was the natural food of the Chinaman, and that where the "pusley" was there would the Chinaman be also. For his part, he welcomed the Chinese emigration: we needed the Chinaman in our gardens to eat the "pusley;" and he thought the whole problem solved by this simple consideration. To get rid of rats and "pusley," he said, was a necessity of our civilization. He did not care so much about the shoe-business; he did not think that the little Chinese shoes that he had seen would be of service in the army: but the garden-interest was quite another affair. We want to make a garden of our whole country: the hoe, in the hands of a man truly great, he was pleased to say, was mightier than the pen. He presumed that Gen. B—tl—r had never taken into consideration the garden-question, or he would not assume the position he does with regard to the Chinese emigration. He would let the Chinese come, even if B—tl—r had to leave, I thought he was going to say, but I changed the subject.

During our entire garden interview (operatically speaking, the garden-scene), the president was not smoking. I do not know how the impression arose that he "uses tobacco in any form;" for I have seen him several times, and he was not smoking. Indeed, I offered him a Connecticut six; but he wittily said that he did not like a weed in a garden,—a remark which I took to have a personal political bearing, and changed the subject.

The president was a good deal surprised at the method and fine appearance of my garden, and to learn that I had the sole care of it. He asked me if I pursued an original course, or whether I got my ideas from writers on the subject. I told him that I had had no time to read any thing on the subject since I began to hoe, except "Lothair," from which I got my ideas of landscape-gardening; and that I had worked the garden entirely according to my own notions, except that I had borne in mind his injunction, "to fight it out on this line if "— The president stopped me abruptly, and said it was unnecessary to repeat that remark: he thought he had heard it before. Indeed, he deeply regretted that he had ever made it. Sometimes, he said, after hearing it in speeches, and coming across it in resolutions, and reading it in newspapers, and having it dropped jocularly by facetious politicians, who were boring him for an office, about twenty-five times a day, say for a month, it would get to running through his head, like the "shoo-fly" song which B—tl—r sings in the House, until it did seem as if he should go distracted. He said, no man could stand that kind of sentence hammering on his brain for years.

The president was so much pleased with my management of the garden, that he offered me (at least, I so understood him) the position of head gardener at the White House, to have care of the exotics. I told him that I thanked him, but that I did not desire any foreign appointment. I had resolved, when the administration came in, not to take an appointment; and I had kept my resolution. As to any home office, I was poor, but honest; and, of course, it would be useless for me to take one. The president mused a moment, and then smiled, and said he would see what could be done for me. I did not change the subject; but nothing further was said by Gen. Gr—nt.

The president is a great talker (contrary to the general impression); but I think he appreciated his quiet hour in my garden. He said it carried him back to his youth farther than any thing he had seen lately. He looked forward with delight to the time when he could again have his private garden, grow his own lettuce and tomatoes, and not have to get so much "sarce" from Congress.

The chair in which the president sat, while declining to take a glass of lager, I have had destroyed, in order that no one may sit in it. It was the only way to save it, if I may so speak. It would have been impossible to keep it from use by any precautions. There are people who would have sat in it, if the seat had been set with iron spikes. Such is the adoration of Station.

NINTH WEEK

I am more and more impressed with the moral qualities of vegetables, and contemplate forming a science which shall rank with comparative anatomy and comparative philology,—the science of comparative vegetable morality. We live in an age of protoplasm. And, if life-matter is essentially the same in all forms of life, I purpose to begin early, and ascertain the nature of the plants for which I am responsible. I will not associate with any vegetable which is disreputable, or has not some quality that can contribute to my moral growth. I do not care to be seen much with the squashes or the dead-beets. Fortunately I can cut down any sorts I do not like with the hoe, and, probably, commit no more sin in so doing, than the Christians did in hewing down the Jews in the middle ages.

This matter of vegetable rank has not been at all studied as it should be. Why do we respect some vegetables, and despise others, when all of them come to an equal honor or ignominy on the table? The bean is a graceful, confiding, engaging vine; but you never can put beans into poetry, nor into the highest sort of prose. There is no dignity in the bean. Corn, which, in my garden, grows alongside the bean, and, so far as I can see, with no affectation of superiority, is, however, the child of song. It waves in all literature. But mix it with beans, and its high tone is gone. Succotash is vulgar. It is the bean in it. The bean is a vulgar vegetable, without culture, or any flavor of high society among vegetables. Then there is the cool cucumber, like so many people,—good for nothing when it is ripe and the wildness has gone out of it. How inferior in quality it is to the melon, which grows upon a similar vine, is of a like watery consistency, but is not half so valuable! The cucumber is a sort of low comedian in a company where the melon is a minor gentleman. I might also contrast the celery with the potato. The associations are as opposite as the dining-room of the duchess and the cabin of the peasant. I admire the potato, both in vine and blossom; but it is not aristocratic. I began digging my potatoes, by the way, about the 4th of July; and I fancy I have discovered the right way to do it. I treat the potato just as I would a cow. I do not pull them up, and shake them out, and destroy them; but I dig carefully at the side of the hill, remove the fruit which is grown, leaving the vine undisturbed: and my theory is, that it will go on bearing, and submitting to my exactions, until the frost cuts it down. It is a game that one would not undertake with a vegetable of tone.

The lettuce is to me a most interesting study. Lettuce is like conversation: it must be fresh and crisp, so sparkling, that you scarcely notice the bitter in it. Lettuce, like most talkers, is, however, apt to run rapidly to seed. Blessed is that sort which comes to a head, and so remains, like a few people I know; growing more solid and satisfactory and tender at the same time, and whiter at the centre, and crisp in their maturity. Lettuce, like conversation, requires a good deal of oil, to avoid friction, and keep the company smooth; a pinch of attic salt; a dash of pepper; a quantity of mustard and vinegar, by all means, but so mixed that you will notice no sharp contrasts; and a trifle of sugar. You can put any thing, and the more things the better, into salad, as into a conversation; but every thing depends upon the skill of mixing. I feel that I am in the best society when I am with lettuce. It is in the select circle of vegetables. The tomato appears well on the table; but you do not want to ask its origin. It is a most agreeable *parvenu*. Of course, I have said nothing about the berries. They live in another and more ideal region; except, perhaps, the currant. Here we see, that, even among berries, there are degrees of breeding. The currant is well enough, clear as truth, and exquisite in color; but I ask you to notice how far it is from the exclusive *hauteur* of the aristocratic strawberry, and the native refinement of the quietly elegant raspberry.

I do not know that chemistry, searching for protoplasm, is able to discover the tendency of vegetables. It can only be found out by outward observation. I confess that I am suspicious of the bean, for instance. There are signs in it of an unregulated life. I put up the most attractive sort of poles for my Limas. They stand high and straight, like church-spires, in my theological garden,— lifted up; and some of them have even budded, like Aaron's rod. No church-steeple in a New-England village was ever better fitted to draw to it the rising generation on Sunday, than those poles to lift up my beans towards heaven. Some of them did run up the sticks seven feet, and then straggled off into the air in a wanton manner; but more than half of them went galivanting off to the neighboring grape-trellis, and wound their tendrils with the tendrils of the grape, with a disregard of the proprieties of life which is a satire upon human nature. And the grape is morally no better. I think the ancients, who were not troubled with the recondite mystery of protoplasm, were right in the mythic union of Bacchus and Venus.

Talk about the Darwinian theory of development, and the principle of natural selection! I should like to see a garden let to run in accordance with it. If I had left my vegetables and weeds to a free fight, in which the strongest specimens only should come to maturity, and the weaker go to the wall, I can clearly see that I should have had a pretty mess of it. It would have been a scene of passion and license and brutality. The "pusley" would have strangled the strawberry; the upright corn, which has now ears to hear the guilty beating of the hearts of the children who steal the raspberries, would have been dragged to the earth by the wandering bean; the snake-grass would have left no place for the potatoes under ground; and the tomatoes would have been swamped by the lusty weeds. With a firm hand, I have had to make my own "natural selection." Nothing will so well bear watching as a garden, except a family of children next door. Their power of selection beats mine. If they could read half as well as they can steal a while away, I should put up a notice, *"Children, beware! There is Protoplasm here."* But I suppose it would have no effect. I believe they would eat protoplasm as quick as any thing else, ripe or green. I wonder if this is going to be a cholera-year. Considerable cholera is the only thing that would let my apples and pears ripen. Of course I do not care for the fruit; but I do not want to take the responsibility of letting so much "life-matter," full of crude and even wicked vegetable-human tendencies, pass into the composition of the neighbors' children, some of whom may be as immortal as snake-grass. There ought to be a public meeting about this, and resolutions, and perhaps a clam-bake. At least, it ought to be put into the catechism, and put in strong.

TENTH WEEK

I think I have discovered the way to keep peas from the birds. I tried the scare-crow plan, in a way which I thought would out-wit the shrewdest bird. The brain of the bird is not large; but it is all concentrated on one object, and that is the attempt to elude the devices of modern civilization which injure his chances of food. I knew, that, if I put up a complete stuffed man, the bird would detect the imitation at once: the perfection of the thing would show him that it was a trick. People always overdo the matter when they attempt deception. I therefore hung some loose garments, of a bright color, upon a rake-head, and set them up among the vines. The supposition was, that the bird would think there was an effort to trap him, that there was a man be-hind, holding up these garments, and would sing, as he kept at a distance, "You can't catch me with any such double device." The bird would know, or think he knew, that I would not hang up such a scare, in the expectation that it would pass for a man, and deceive a bird; and he would therefore look for a deeper plot. I expected to out-wit the bird by a duplicity that was simplicity itself. I may have over-calculated the sagacity and reasoning power of the bird. At any rate, I did over-calculate the amount of peas I should gather.

But my game was only half played. In another part of the garden were other peas, growing and blowing. To these I took good care not to attract the attention of the bird by any scare-crow whatever! I left the old scare-crow conspicuously flaunting above the old vines; and by this means I hope to keep the attention of the birds confined to that side of the garden. I am convinced that this is the true use of a scare-crow: it is a lure, and not a warning. If you wish to save men from any particular vice, set up a tremendous cry of warning about some other; and they will all give their special efforts to the one to which attention is called. This profound truth is about the only thing I have yet realized out of my pea-vines.

However, the garden does begin to yield. I know of nothing that makes one feel more complacent, in these July days, than to have his vegetables from his own garden. What an effect it has on the market-man and the butcher! It is a kind of declaration of independence. The market-man shows me his peas and beets and tomatoes, and supposes he shall send me out some with the meat. "No, I thank you," I say carelessly: "I am raising my own this year." Whereas I have been wont to remark, "Your vegetables look a little wilted this weather," I now say, "What a fine lot of vegetables you've got!" When a man is not going to buy, he can afford to be generous. To raise his own vegetables makes a person feel, somehow, more liberal. I think the butcher is touched by the influence, and cuts off a better roast for me. The butcher is my friend when he sees that I am not wholly dependent on him.

It is at home, however, that the effect is most marked, though sometimes in a way that I had not expected. I have never read of any Roman supper that seemed to me equal to a dinner of my own vegetables; when every thing on the table is the product of my own labor, except the clams, which I have not been able to raise yet, and the chickens, which have withdrawn from the garden just when they were most attractive. It is strange what a taste you suddenly have for things you never liked before. The squash has always been to me a dish of contempt; but I eat it now as if it were my best friend. I never cared for the beet or the bean; but I fancy now that I could eat them all, tops and all, so completely have they been transformed by the soil in which they grew. I think the squash is less squashy, and the beet has a deeper hue of rose, for my care of them.

I had begun to nurse a good deal of pride in presiding over a table whereon was the fruit of my honest industry. But woman!—John Stuart Mill is right when he says that we do not know any thing about women. Six thousand years is as one day with them. I thought I had something to do with those vegetables. But when I saw Polly seated at her side of the table, presiding over the new and susceptible vegetables, flanked by the squash and the beans, and smiling upon the green corn and the new potatoes, as cool as the cucumbers which lay sliced in ice before her, and when she began to dispense the fresh dishes, I saw at once that the day of my destiny was over. You would have thought that she owned all the vegetables, and had raised them all from their earliest years. Such quiet, vegetable airs! Such gracious appropriation! At length I said,—

"Polly, do you know who planted that squash, or those squashes?"

"James, I suppose."

"Well, yes, perhaps James did plant them, to a certain extent. But who hoed them?"

"We did."

"*We* did!" I said in the most sarcastic manner. "And I suppose *we* put on the sack-cloth and ashes, when the striped bug came at four o'clock, A.M., and we watched the tender leaves, and watered night and morning the feeble plants. I tell you, Polly," said I, uncorking the Bordeaux raspberry vinegar, "there is not a pea here that does not represent a drop of moisture wrung from my brow, not a beet that does not stand for a back-ache, not a squash that has not caused me untold anxiety; and I did hope—but I will say no more."

Observation.—In this sort of family discussion, "I will say no more" is the most effective thing you can close up with.

I am not an alarmist. I hope I am as cool as anybody this hot summer. But I am quite ready to say to Polly, or any other woman, "You can have the ballot; only leave me the vegetables, or, what is more important, the consciousness of power in vegetables." I see how it is. Woman is now supreme in the house. She already stretches out her hand to grasp the garden. She will gradually control every thing. Woman is one of the ablest and most cunning creatures who have ever mingled in human affairs. I understand those women who say they don't want the ballot. They purpose to hold the real power, while we go through the mockery of making laws. They want the power without the responsibility. (Suppose my squash had not come up, or my beans—as they threatened at one time—had gone the wrong way: where would I have been?) We are to be held to all the responsibilities. Woman takes the lead in all the departments, leaving us politics only. And what is politics? Let me raise the vegetables of a nation, says Polly, and I care not who makes its politics. Here I sat at the table, armed with the ballot, but really powerless among my own vegetables. While we are being amused by the ballot, woman is quietly taking things into her own hands.

Eleventh Week

Perhaps, after all, it is not what you get out of a garden, but what you put into it, that is the most remunerative. What is a man? A question frequently asked, and never, so far as I know, satisfactorily answered. He commonly spends his seventy years, if so many are given him, in getting ready to enjoy himself. How many hours, how many minutes, does one get of that pure content which is happiness? I do not mean laziness, which is always discontent; but that serene enjoyment, in which all the natural senses have easy play, and the unnatural ones have a holiday. There is probably nothing that has such a tranquillizing effect, and leads into such content, as gardening. By gardening, I do not mean that insane desire to raise vegetables which some have; but the philosophical occupation of contact with the earth, and companionship with gently growing things and patient processes; that exercise which soothes the spirit, and develops the deltoid muscles.

In half an hour I can hoe myself right away from this world, as we commonly see it, into a large place where there are no obstacles. What an occupation it is for thought! The mind broods like a hen on eggs. The trouble is, that you are not thinking about any thing, but are really vegetating like the plants around you. I begin to know what the joy of the grape-vine is in running up the trellis, which is similar to that of the squirrel in running up a tree. We all have something in our nature that requires contact with the earth. In the solitude of garden-labor, one gets into a sort of communion with the vegetable life, which makes the old mythology possible. For instance, I can believe that the dryads are plenty this summer: my garden is like an ash-heap. Almost all the moisture it has had in weeks has been the sweat of honest industry.

The pleasure of gardening in these days, when the thermometer is at ninety, is one that I fear I shall not be able to make intelligible to my readers, many of whom do not appreciate the delight of soaking in the sunshine. I suppose that the sun, going through a man, as it will on such a day, takes out of him rheumatism, consumption, and every other disease, except sudden death—from sun-stroke. But, aside from this, there is an odor from the evergreens, the hedges, the various plants and vines, that is only expressed and set afloat at a high temperature, which is delicious; and, hot as it may be, a little breeze will come at intervals, which can be heard in the tree-tops, and which is an unobtrusive benediction. I hear a quail or two whistling in the ravine; and there is a good deal of fragmentary conversation going on among the birds, even on the warmest days. The companionship of Calvin, also, counts for a good deal. He usually attends me, unless I work too long in one place; sitting down on the turf, displaying the ermine of his breast, and watching my movements with great intelligence. He has a feline and genuine love for the beauties of Nature, and will establish himself where there is a good view, and look on it for hours. He always accompanies us when we go to gather the vegetables, seeming to be desirous to know what we are to have for dinner. He is a connoisseur in the garden; being fond of almost all the vegetables, except the cucumber,—a dietetic hint to man. I believe it is also said that the pig will not eat tobacco. These are important facts. It is singular, however, that those who hold up the pigs as models to us never hold us up as models to the pigs.

I wish I knew as much about natural history and the habits of animals as Calvin does. He is the closest observer I ever saw; and there are few species of animals on the place that he has not analyzed. I think that he has, to use a euphemism very applicable to him, got outside of every one of them, except the toad. To the toad he is entirely indifferent; but I presume he knows that the toad is the most useful animal in the garden. I think the Agricultural Society ought to offer a prize for the finest toad. When Polly comes to sit in the shade near my strawberry-beds, to shell peas, Calvin is always lying near in apparent obliviousness; but not the slightest unusual sound can be made in the bushes, that he is not alert, and prepared to investigate the cause of it. It is this habit of observation, so cultivated, which has given him such a trained mind, and made him so philosophical. It is within the capacity of even the humblest of us to attain this.

And, speaking of the philosophical temper, there is no class of men whose society is more to be desired for this quality than that of plumbers. They are the most agreeable men I know; and the boys in the business begin to be agreeable very early. I suspect the secret of it is, that they are agreeable by the hour. In the dryest days, my fountain became disabled: the pipe was stopped up. A couple of plumbers, with the implements of their craft, came out to view the situation. There was a good deal of difference of opinion about where the stoppage was. I found the plumbers perfectly willing to sit down and talk about it,—talk by the hour. Some of their guesses and remarks were exceedingly ingenious; and their general observations on other subjects were excellent in their way, and could hardly have been better if they had been made by the job. The work dragged a little—as it is apt to do by the hour. The plumbers had occasion to make me several visits. Sometimes they would find, upon arrival, that they had forgotten some indispensable tool; and one would go back to the shop, a mile and a half, after it; and his comrade would await his return with the most exemplary patience, and sit down and talk,—always by the hour. I do not know but it is a habit to have something wanted at the shop. They seemed to me very good workmen, and always willing to stop and talk about the job, or any thing else, when I went near them. Nor had they any of that impetuous hurry that is said to be the bane of our American civilization. To their credit be it said, that I never observed any thing of it in them. They can afford to wait. Two of them will sometimes wait nearly half a day while a comrade goes for a tool. They are patient and philosophical. It is a great pleasure to meet such men. One only wishes there was some work he could do for *them* by the hour. There ought to be reciprocity. I think they have very nearly solved the problem of Life: it is to work for other people, never for yourself, and get your pay by the hour. You then have no anxiety, and little work. If you do things by the job, you are perpetually driven: the hours are scourges. If you work by the hour, you gently sail on the stream of Time, which is always bearing you on to the haven of Pay, whether you make any effort, or not. Working by the hour tends to make one moral. A plumber working by the job, trying to unscrew a rusty, refractory nut, in a cramped position, where the tongs continually slipped off, would swear; but I never heard one of them swear, or exhibit the least impatience at such a vexation, working by the hour. Nothing can move a man who is paid by the hour. How sweet the flight of time seems to his calm mind!

TWELFTH WEEK

Mr. Horace Greeley, the introduction of whose name confers an honor upon this page (although I ought to say that it is used entirely without his consent), is my sole authority in agriculture. In politics, I do not dare to follow him; but in agriculture he is irresistible. When, therefore, I find him advising Western farmers not to hill up their corn, I think that his advice must be political. You must hill up your corn. People always have hilled up their corn. It would take a constitutional amendment to change the practice, that has pertained ever since maize was raised. "It will stand the drought better," says Mr. Greeley, "if the ground is left level." I have corn in my garden, ten and twelve feet high, strong and lusty, standing the drought like a grenadier; and it is hilled. In advising this radical change, Mr. Greeley evidently has a political purpose. He might just as well say that you should not hill beans, when everybody knows that a "hill of beans" is one of the most expressive symbols of disparagement When I become too lazy to hill my corn, I, too, shall go into politics.

I am satisfied that it is useless to try to cultivate "pusley." I set a little of it to one side, and gave it some extra care. It did not thrive as well as that which I was fighting. The fact is, there is a spirit of moral perversity in the plant, which makes it grow the more, the more it is interfered with. I am satisfied of that. I doubt if any one has raised more "pusley" this year than I have; and my warfare with it has been continual. Neither of us has slept much. If you combat it, it will grow, to use an expression that will be understood by many, like the devil. I have a neighbor, a good Christian man, benevolent, and a person of good judgment. He planted next to me an acre of turnips recently. A few days after, he went to look at his crop; and he found the entire ground covered with a thick and luxurious carpet of "pusley," with a turnip-top worked in here and there as an ornament. I have seldom seen so thrifty a field. I advised my neighbor next time to sow "pusley;" and then he might get a few turnips. I wish there was more demand in our city markets for "pusley" as a salad. I can recommend it.

It does not take a great man to soon discover, that, in raising any thing, the greater part of the plants goes into stalk and leaf, and the fruit is a most inconsiderable portion. I plant and hoe a hill of corn: it grows green and stout, and waves its broad leaves high in the air, and is months in perfecting itself, and then yields us not enough for a dinner. It grows because it delights to do so,—to take the juices out of my ground, to absorb my fertilizers, to wax luxuriant, and disport itself in the summer air, and with very little thought of making any return to me. I might go all through my garden and fruit-trees with a similar result. I have heard of places where there was very little land to the acre. It is universally true, that there is a great deal of vegetable show and fuss for the result produced. I do not complain of this. One cannot expect vegetables to be better than men: and they make a great deal of ostentatious splurge; and many of them come to no result at last. Usually, the more show of leaf and wood, the less fruit. This melancholy reflection is thrown in here in order to make dog-days seem cheerful in comparison.

One of the minor pleasures of life is that of controlling vegetable activity and aggressions with the pruning-knife. Vigorous and rapid growth is, however, a necessity to the sport. To prune feeble plants and shrubs is like acting the part of dry-nurse to a sickly orphan. You must feel the blood of Nature bound under your hand, and get the thrill of its life in your nerves. To control and culture a strong, thrifty plant, in this way, is like steering a ship under full headway, or driving a locomotive with your hand on the lever, or pulling the reins over a fast horse when his blood and tail are up. I do not understand, by the way, the pleasure of the jockey in setting up the tail of the horse artificially. If I had a horse with a tail not able to sit up, I should feed the horse, and curry him into good spirits, and let him set up his own tail. When I see a poor, spiritless horse going by with an artificially set-up tail, it is only a signal of distress. I desire to be surrounded only by healthy, vigorous plants and trees, which require constant cutting-in and management. Merely to cut away dead branches is like perpetual attendance at a funeral, and puts one in low spirits. I want to have a garden and orchard rise up and meet me every morning, with the request to "lay on, Macduff." I respect old age; but an old currant-bush, hoary with mossy bark, is a melancholy spectacle.

I suppose the time has come when I am expected to say something about fertilizers: all agriculturists do. When you plant, you think you cannot fertilize too much: when you get the bills for the manure, you think you cannot fertilize too little. Of course, you do not expect to get the value of the manure back in fruits and vegetables; but something is due to science,— to chemistry in particular. You must have a knowledge of soils, must have your soil analyzed, and then go into a course of experiments to find what it needs. It needs analyzing,—that, I am clear about: every thing needs that. You had better have the soil analyzed before you buy: if there is "pusley" in it, let it alone. See if it is a soil that requires much hoeing, and how fine it will get if there is no rain for two months. But when you come to fertilizing, if I understand the agricultural authorities, you open a pit that will ultimately swallow you up,—farm and all. It is the great subject of modern times, how to fertilize without ruinous expense; how, in short, not to starve the earth to death while we get our living out of it. Practically, the business is hardly to the taste of a person of a poetic turn of mind. The details of fertilizing are not agreeable. Michael Angelo, who tried every art, and nearly every trade, never gave his mind to fertilizing. It is much pleasanter and easier to fertilize with a pen, as the agricultural writers do, than with a fork. And this leads me to say, that, in carrying on a garden yourself, you must have a "consulting" gardener; that is, a man to do the heavy and unpleasant work. To such a man, I say, in language used by Demosthenes to the Athenians, and which is my advice to all gardeners, "Fertilize, fertilize, fertilize!"

THIRTEENTH WEEK

I find that gardening has unsurpassed advantages for the study of natural history; and some scientific facts have come under my own observation, which cannot fail to interest naturalists and un-naturalists in about the same degree. Much, for instance, has been written about the toad, an animal without which no garden would be complete. But little account has been made of his value: the beauty of his eye alone has been dwelt on; and little has been said of his mouth, and its important function as a fly and bug trap. His habits, and even his origin, have been misunderstood. Why, as an illustration, are toads so plenty after a thunder-shower? All my life long, no one has been able to answer me that question. Why after a heavy shower, and in the midst of it, do such multitudes of toads, especially little ones, hop about on the gravel-walks? For many years, I believed that they rained down; and I suppose many people think so still.

They are so small, and they come in such numbers only in the shower, that the supposition is not a violent one. "Thick as toads after a shower," is one of our best proverbs. I asked an explanation of this of a thoughtful woman,—indeed, a leader in the great movement to have all the toads hop in any direction, without any distinction of sex or religion. Her reply was, that the toads come out during the shower to get water. This, however, is not the fact. I have discovered that they come out not to get water. I deluged a dry flower-bed, the other night, with pailful after pailful of water. Instantly the toads came out of their holes in the dirt, by tens and twenties and fifties, to escape death by drowning. The big ones fled away in a ridiculous streak of hopping; and the little ones sprang about in the wildest confusion. The toad is just like any other land animal: when his house is full of water, he quits it. These facts, with the drawings of the water and the toads, are at the service of the distinguished scientists of Albany in New York, who were so much impressed by the Cardiff Giant.

The domestic cow is another animal whose ways I have a chance to study, and also to obliterate in the garden. One of my neighbors has a cow, but no land; and he seems desirous to pasture her on the surface of the land of other people: a very reasonable desire. The man proposed that he should be allowed to cut the grass from my grounds for his cow. I knew the cow, having often had her in my garden; knew her gait and the size of her feet, which struck me as a little large for the size of the body. Having no cow myself, but acquaintance with my neighbor's, I told him that I thought it would be fair for him to have the grass. He was, therefore, to keep the grass nicely cut, and to keep his cow at home. I waited some time after the grass needed cutting;

and, as my neighbor did not appear, I hired it cut. No sooner was it done, than he promptly appeared, and raked up most of it, and carried it away. He had evidently been waiting that opportunity. When the grass grew again, the neighbor did not appear with his scythe; but one morning I found the cow tethered on the sward, hitched near the clothes-horse, a short distance from the house. This seemed to be the man's idea of the best way to cut the grass. I disliked to have the cow there, because I knew her inclination to pull up the stake, and transfer her field of mowing to the garden, but especially because of her voice. She has the most melancholy "moo" I ever heard. It is like the wail of one un-infallible, excommunicated, and lost. It is a most distressing perpetual reminder of the brevity of life and the shortness of feed. It is unpleasant to the family. We sometimes hear it in the middle of the night, breaking the silence like a suggestion of coming calamity. It is as bad as the howling of a dog at a funeral.

I told the man about it; but he seemed to think that he was not responsible for the cow's voice. I then told him to take her away; and he did, at intervals, shifting her to different parts of the grounds in my absence, so that the desolate voice would startle us from unexpected quarters. If I were to unhitch the cow, and turn her loose, I knew where she would go. If I were to lead her away, the question was, Where? for I did not fancy leading a cow about till I could find somebody who was willing to pasture her. To this dilemma had my excellent neighbor reduced me. But I found him, one Sunday morning,—a day when it would not do to get angry,—tying his cow at the foot of the hill; the beast all the time going on in that abominable voice. I told the man that I could not have the cow in the grounds. He said, "All right, boss;" but he did not go away. I asked him to clear out. The man, who is a French sympathizer from the Republic of Ireland, kept his temper perfectly. He said he wasn't doing any thing, just feeding his cow a bit: he wouldn't make me the least trouble in the world. I reminded him that he had been told again and again not to come here; that he might have all the grass, but he should not bring his cow upon the premises. The imperturbable man assented to every thing that I said, and kept on feeding his cow. Before I got him to go to fresh scenes and pastures new, the sabbath was almost broken: but it was saved by one thing; it is difficult to be emphatic when no one is emphatic on the other side. The man and his cow have taught me a great lesson, which I shall recall when I keep a cow. I can recommend this cow, if anybody wants one, as a steady boarder, whose keeping will cost the owner little; but, if her milk is at all like her voice, those who drink it are on the straight road to lunacy.

I think I have said that we have a game-preserve. We keep quails, or try to, in the thickly wooded, bushed, and brushed ravine. This bird is a great favorite with us, dead or alive, on account of its tasteful plumage, its tender flesh, its domestic virtues, and its pleasant piping. Besides, although I appreciate toads and cows, and all that sort of thing, I like to have a game-preserve more in the English style. And we did. For in July, while the game-law was on, and the young quails were coming on, we were awakened one morning by firing,—musketry-firing, close at hand. My first thought was, that war was declared; but, as I should never pay much attention to war declared at that time in the morning, I went to sleep again. But the occurrence was repeated,—and not only early in the morning, but at night. There was calling of dogs, breaking down of brush, and firing of guns. It is hardly pleasant to have guns fired in the direction of the house, at your own quails. The hunters could be sometimes seen, but never caught. Their best time was about sunrise; but, before one could dress and get to the front, they would retire.

One morning, about four o'clock, I heard the battle renewed. I sprang up, but not in arms, and went to a window. Polly (like another "blessed damozel") flew to another window,—

> "The blessed damozel leaned out
> From the gold bar of heaven,"—

and reconnoitred from behind the blinds.

> "The wonder was not yet quite gone
> From that still look of hers,"

when an armed man and a legged dog appeared in the opening. I was vigilantly watching him.

> "And now
> She spoke through the still weather."

"Are you afraid to speak to him?" asked Polly. Not exactly,

> "she spoke as when
> The stars sang in their spheres."

Stung by this inquiry, I leaned out of the window till

> "The bar *I* leaned on (was) warm,"

and cried,—

"Halloo, there! What are you doing?"

"Look out he don't shoot you," called out Polly from the other window, suddenly going on another tack.

I explained, that a sportsman would not be likely to shoot a gentleman in his own house, with bird-shot, so long as quails were to be had.

"You have no business here: what are you after?" I repeated.

"Looking for a lost hen," said the man as he strode away.

The reply was so satisfactory and conclusive, that I shut the blinds, and went to bed.

But one evening I overhauled one of the poachers. Hearing his dog in the thicket, I rushed through the brush, and came in sight of the hunter as he was retreating down the road. He came to a halt; and we had some conversation in a high key. Of course, I threatened to prosecute him. I believe that is the thing to do in such cases; but how I was to do it, when I did not know his name or ancestry, and couldn't see his face, never occurred to me. (I remember, now, that a farmer once proposed to prosecute me when I was fishing in a trout-brook on his farm, and asked my name for that purpose.) He said he should smile to see me prosecute him.

"You can't do it: there ain't no notice up about trespassing." This view of the common law impressed me; and I said,—

"But these are private grounds."

"Private h—!" was all his response.

You can't argue much with a man who has a gun in his hands, when you have none. Besides, it might be a needle-gun, for aught I knew. I gave it up, and we separated.

There is this disadvantage about having a game-preserve attached to your garden: it makes life too lively.

FOURTEENTH WEEK

In these golden latter August days, Nature has come to a serene equilibrium. Having flowered and fruited, she is enjoying herself. I can see how things are going: it is a down-hill business after this; but, for the time being, it is like swinging in a hammock,—such a delicious air, such a graceful repose! I take off my hat as I stroll into the garden and look about; and it does seem as if Nature had sounded a truce. I didn't ask for it. I went out with a hoe; but the serene sweetness disarms me. Thrice is he armed who has a long-handled-hoe, with a double blade. Yet to-day I am almost ashamed to appear in such a belligerent fashion, with this terrible mitrailleuse of gardening.

The tomatoes are getting tired of ripening, and are beginning to go into a worthless condition,—green. The cucumbers cumber the ground,—great yellow, over-ripe objects, no more to be compared to the crisp beauty of their youth than is the fat swine of the sty to the clean little pig. The nutmeg-melons, have covered themselves with delicate lace-work, are now ready to leave the vine. I know they are ripe if they come easily off the stem.

Moral Observations.—You can tell when people are ripe by their willingness to let go. Richness and ripeness are not exactly the same. The rich are apt to hang to the stem with tenacity. I have nothing against the rich. If I were not virtuous, I should like to be rich. But we cannot have every thing, as the man said when he was down with small-pox and cholera, and the yellow-fever came into the neighborhood.

Now, the grapes, soaked in this liquid gold, called air, begin to turn, mindful of the injunction, "to turn or burn." The clusters under the leaves are getting quite purple, but look better than they taste. I think there is no danger but they will be gathered as soon as they are ripe. One of the blessings of having an open garden is, that I do not have to watch my fruit: a dozen youngsters do that, and let it waste no time after it matures. I wish it were possible to grow a variety of grape like the explosive bullets, that should explode in the stomach: the vine would make such a nice border for the garden,—a masked battery of grape. The pears, too, are getting russet and heavy; and here and there amid the shining leaves, one gleams as ruddy as the cheek of the Nut-brown Maid. The Flemish Beauties come off readily from the stem, if I take them in my hand: they say all kinds of beauty come off by handling.

The garden is peace as much as if it were an empire. Even the man's cow lies down under the tree where the man has tied her, with such an air of contentment, that I have small desire to disturb her. She is chewing my cud as if it were hers. Well, eat on

...d chew on, melancholy brute. I have not the heart to tell the man to take you away: and it would do no good if I had; he wouldn't do it. The man has not a taking way. Munch on, ruminant creature. The frost will soon come; the grass will be brown. I will be charitable while this blessed lull continues; for our benevolences must soon be turned to other and more distant objects,—the amelioration of the condition of the Jews, the education of theological young men in the West, and the like.

I do not know that these appearances are deceitful; but I sufficiently know that this is a wicked world, to be glad that I have taken it on shares. In fact, I could not pick the pears alone, not to speak of eating them. When I climb the trees, and throw down the dusky fruit, Polly catches it in her apron; nearly always, however, letting go when it drops, the fall is so sudden. The sun gets in her face; and, every time a pear comes down, it is a surprise, like having a tooth out, she says.

"If I couldn't hold an apron better than that!"— But the sentence is not finished: it is useless to finish that sort of a sentence in this delicious weather. Besides, conversation is dangerous. As, for instance, towards evening I am preparing a bed for a sowing of turnips,—not that I like turnips in the least; but this is the season to sow them. Polly comes out, and extemporizes her usual seat to "consult me" about matters while I work. I well know that something is coming.

"This is a rotation of crops, isn't it?"

"Yes: I have rotated the gone-to-seed lettuce off, and expect to rotate the turnips in; it is a political fashion."

"Isn't it a shame that the tomatoes are all getting ripe at once? What a lot of squashes! I wish we had an oyster-bed. Do you want me to help you any more than I am helping?"

"No, I thank you." (I wonder what all this is about?)

"Don't you think we could sell some strawberries next y

"By all means, sell any thing. We shall no doubt get rich out
this acre."

"Don't be foolish."

And now!

"Don't you think it would be nice to have a?"— And Polly unfolds a small scheme of benevolence, which is not quite enough
to break me, and is really to be executed in an economical manner. "Wouldn't that be nice?"

"Oh, yes! And where is the money to come from?"

"I thought we had agreed to sell the strawberries."

"Certainly. But I think we would make more money if we sold
the plants now."

"Well," said Polly, concluding the whole matter, "I am going
to do it." And, having thus "consulted" me, Polly goes away; and
I put in the turnip-seeds quite thick, determined to raise enough
to sell. But not even this mercenary thought can ruffle my mind
as I rake off the loamy bed. I notice, however, that the spring
smell has gone out of the dirt. That went into the first crop.

In this peaceful unison with yielding nature, I was a little
taken aback to find that a new enemy had turned up. The celery
had just rubbed through the fiery scorching of the drought, and
stood a faint chance to grow; when I noticed on the green leaves
a big green-and-black worm, called, I believe, the celery-worm:
but I don't know who called him; I am sure I did not. It was almost ludicrous that he should turn up here, just at the end of the
season, when I supposed that my war with the living animals was
over. Yet he was, no doubt, predestinated; for he went to work
as cheerfully as if he had arrived in June, when every thing was
fresh and vigorous. It beats me—Nature does. I doubt not, that,
if I were to leave my garden now for a week, it wouldn't know

n my return. The patch I scratched over for the turnips, and t as clean as earth, is already full of ambitious "pusley," which grows with all the confidence of youth and the skill of old age. It beats the serpent as an emblem of immortality. While all the others of us in the garden rest and sit in comfort a moment, upon the summit of the summer, it is as rampant and vicious as ever. It accepts no armistice.

FIFTEENTH WEEK

It is said that absence conquers all things, love included; but it has a contrary effect on a garden. I was absent for two or three weeks. I left my garden a paradise, as paradises go in this proto-plasmic world; and, when I returned, the trail of the serpent was over it all, so to speak. (This is in addition to the actual snakes in it, which are large enough to strangle children of average size.) I asked Polly if she had seen to the garden while I was away, and she said she had. I found that all the melons had been seen to, and the early grapes and pears. The green worm had also seen to about half the celery; and a large flock of apparently perfectly domesticated chickens were roaming over the ground, gossiping in the hot September sun, and picking up any odd trifle that might be left. On the whole, the garden could not have been better seen to; though it would take a sharp eye to see the potato-vines amid the rampant grass and weeds.

_e_ new strawberry-plants, for one thing, had taken advan-
__ of my absence. Every one of them had sent out as many
arlet runners as an Indian tribe has. Some of them had blossomed; and a few had gone so far as to bear ripe berries,—long,
pear-shaped fruit, hanging like the ear-pendants of an East-
Indian bride. I could not but admire the persistence of these
zealous plants, which seemed determined to propagate themselves both by seeds and roots, and make sure of immortality in
some way. Even the Colfax variety was as ambitious as the others. After having seen the declining letter of Mr. Colfax, I did
not suppose that this vine would run any more, and intended to
root it out. But one can never say what these politicians mean;
and I shall let this variety grow until after the next election, at
least; although I hear that the fruit is small, and rather sour. If
there is any variety of strawberries that really declines to run,
and devotes itself to a private life of fruit-bearing, I should like
to get it. I may mention here, since we are on politics, that the
Doolittle raspberries had sprawled all over the strawberry-beds:
so true is it that politics makes strange bed-fellows.

But another enemy had come into the strawberries, which,
after all that has been said in these papers, I am almost ashamed
to mention. But does the preacher in the pulpit, Sunday after
Sunday, year after year, shrink from speaking of sin? I refer, of
course, to the greatest enemy of mankind, "p-sl-y." The ground
was carpeted with it. I should think that this was the tenth crop
of the season; and it was as good as the first. I see no reason why
our northern soil is not as prolific as that of the tropics, and will
not produce as many crops in the year. The mistake we make is
in trying to force things that are not natural to it. I have no
doubt, that, if we turn our attention to "pusley," we can beat the
world.

I had no idea, until recently, how generally this simple thrifty plant is feared and hated. Far beyond what I had regard as the bounds of civilization, it is held as one of the mysteries a fallen world; accompanying the home missionary on his wanderings, and preceding the footsteps of the Tract Society. I was, not long ago, in the Adirondacks. We had built a camp for the night, in the heart of the woods, high up on John's Brook, and near the foot of Mount Marcy: I can see the lovely spot now. It was on the bank of the crystal, rocky stream, at the foot of high and slender falls, which poured into a broad amber basin. Out of this basin we had just taken trout enough for our supper, which had been killed, and roasted over the fire on sharp sticks, and eaten before they had an opportunity to feel the chill of this deceitful world. We were lying under the hut of spruce-bark, on fragrant hemlock-boughs, talking, after supper. In front of us was a huge fire of birch-logs; and over it we could see the top of the falls glistening in the moonlight; and the roar of the falls, and the brawling of the stream near us, filled all the ancient woods. It was a scene upon which one would think no thought of sin could enter. We were talking with old Phelps, the guide. Old Phelps is at once guide, philosopher, and friend. He knows the woods and streams and mountains, and their savage inhabitants, as well as we know all our rich relations, and what they are doing; and, in lonely bear-hunts and sable-trappings, he has thought out and solved most of the problems of life. As he stands in his wood-gear, he is as grizzly as an old cedar-tree; and he speaks in a high falsetto voice, which would be invaluable to a boatswain in a storm at sea.

We had been talking of all subjects about which rational men are interested,—bears, panthers, trapping, the habits of trout, the tariff, the internal revenue (to wit, the injustice of laying tax on tobacco, and none on dogs: "There ain't no dog in Jnited States," says the guide, at the top of his voice, "that arns his living"), the Adventists, the Gorner Grat, Horace Greeley, religion, the propagation of seeds in the wilderness (as, for instance, where were the seeds lying for ages that spring up into certain plants and flowers as soon as a spot is cleared anywhere in the most remote forest; and why does a growth of oak-trees always come up after a growth of pine has been removed?)—in short, we had pretty nearly reached a solution of many mysteries, when Phelps suddenly exclaimed with uncommon energy,—

"Wall, there's one thing that beats me!"

"What's that?" we asked with undisguised curiosity.

"That's 'pusley'!" he replied, in the tone of a man who has come to one door in life which is hopelessly shut, and from which he retires in despair.

"Where it comes from I don't know, nor what to do with it. It's in my garden; and I can't get rid of it. It beats me."

About "pusley" the guide had no theory and no hope. A feeling of awe came over me, as we lay there at midnight, hushed by the sound of the stream and the rising wind in the spruce-tops. Then, man can go nowhere that "pusley" will not attend him. Though he camp on the Upper Au Sable, or penetrate the forest where rolls the Allegash, and hears no sound save his own allegations, he will not escape it. It has entered the happy valley of Keene, although there is yet no church there, and only a feeble school part of the year. Sin travels faster than they that ride in chariots. I take my hoe, and begin; but I feel that I am warring against something whose roots take hold on H.

By the time a man gets to be eighty, he learns that he is compassed by limitations, and that there has been a natural boundary set to his individual powers. As he goes on in life, he begins to doubt his ability to destroy all evil and to reform all abuse, to suspect that there will be much left to do after he has done stepped into my garden in the spring, not doubting that I should be easily master of the weeds. I have simply learned that an institution which is at least six thousand years old, and I believe six millions, is not to be put down in one season.

I have been digging my potatoes, if anybody cares to know it. I planted them in what are called "Early Rose,"—the rows a little less than three feet apart; but the vines came to an early close in the drought. Digging potatoes is a pleasant, soothing occupation, but not poetical. It is good for the mind, unless they are too small (as many of mine are); when it begets a want of gratitude to the bountiful earth. What small potatoes we all are, compared with what we might be! We don't plough deep enough, any of us, for one thing. I shall put in the plough next year, and give the tubers room enough I think they felt the lack of it this year: many of them seemed ashamed to come out so small. There is great pleasure in turning out the brown-jacketed fellows into the sunshine of a royal September day, and seeing them glisten as they lie thickly strewn on the warm soil. Life has few such moments. But then they must be picked up. The picking-up, in this world, is always the unpleasant part of it.

Sixteenth Week

I do not hold myself bound to answer the question, Does gardening pay? It is so difficult to define what is meant by paying. There is a popular notion, that, unless a thing pays, you had better let it alone; and I may say that there is a public opinion that will not let a man or woman continue in the indulgence of a fancy that does not pay. And public opinion is stronger than the legislature, and nearly as strong as the ten commandments: I therefore yield to popular clamor when I discuss the profit of my garden.

As I look at it, you might as well ask, Does a sunset pay? I know that a sunset is commonly looked on as a cheap entertainment; but it is really one of the most expensive. It is true that we can all have front seats, and we do not exactly need to dress for it as we do for the opera; but the conditions under which it is to be enjoyed are rather dear. Among them I should name a good suit of clothes, including some trifling ornament,—not includ-

ing back hair for one sex, or the parting of it in the midd.
the other. I should add also a good dinner, well cooked a.
digestible; and the cost of a fair education, extended, perhaps,
through generations in which sensibility and love of beauty
grew. What I mean is, that if a man is hungry and naked, and half
a savage, or with the love of beauty undeveloped in him, a sunset is thrown away on him: so that it appears that the conditions
of the enjoyment of a sunset are as costly as any thing in our
civilization.

Of course, there is no such thing as absolute value in this
world. You can only estimate what a thing is worth to *you*. Does
gardening in a city pay? You might as well ask if it pays to keep
hens, or a trotting-horse, or to wear a gold ring, or to keep your
lawn cut, or your hair cut. It is as you like it. In a certain sense, it
is a sort of profanation to consider if my garden pays, or to set a
money-value upon my delight in it. I fear that you could not put
it in money. Job had the right idea in his mind, when he asked,
"Is there any taste in the white of an egg?" Suppose there is
not! What! shall I set a price upon the tender asparagus or the
crisp lettuce, which made the sweet spring a reality? Shall I turn
into merchandise the red strawberry, the pale green pea, the
high-flavored raspberry, the sanguinary beet, that love-plant
the tomato, and the corn which did not waste its sweetness on
the desert air, but, after flowing in a sweet rill through all our
summer life, mingled at last with the engaging bean in a pool of
succotash? Shall I compute in figures what daily freshness and
health and delight the garden yields, let alone the large crop
of anticipation I gathered as soon as the first seeds got above
ground? I appeal to any gardening man of sound mind, if that
which pays him best in gardening is not that which he cannot
show in his trial-balance. Yet I yield to public opinion, when I

ced to make such a balance; and I do it with the utmost con-
ence in figures.

I select as a representative vegetable, in order to estimate the
cost of gardening, the potato. In my statement, I shall not in-
clude the interest on the value of the land. I throw in the land,
because it would otherwise have stood idle: the thing generally
raised on city land is taxes. I therefore make the following statement of the cost and income of my potato-crop, a part of it estimated in connection with other garden labor. I have tried to
make it so as to satisfy the income-tax collector:—

	DR.
Ploughing	$0.50
Seed	1.50
Manure	8.00
Assistance in planting and digging, 3 days	6.75
Labor of self in planting, hoeing, digging, picking up, 5 days at 17 cents	.85
TOTAL COST	$17.60
	CR.
Two thousand five hundred mealy potatoes, at 2 cents	$50.00
Small potatoes given to neighbor's pig	.50
TOTAL RETURN	$50.50
BALANCE, profit in cellar	$32.90

Some of these items need explanation. I have charged nothing for my own time waiting for the potatoes to grow. My time in
hoeing, fighting weeds, &c., is put in at five days: it may have
been a little more. Nor have I put in any thing for cooling drinks
while hoeing. I leave this out from principle, because I always
recommend water to others. I had some difficulty in fixing the

rate of my own wages. It was the first time that I had an o
tunity of paying what I thought labor was worth; and I de
mined to make a good thing of it for once. I figured it right dow
to European prices,---seventeen cents a day for unskilled labor.
Of course, I boarded myself. I ought to say that I fixed the wages
after the work was done, or I might have been tempted to do as
some masons did who worked for me at four dollars a day. They
lay in the shade and slept the sleep of honest toil full half the
time,---at least all the time I was away. I have reason to believe,
that when the wages of mechanics are raised to eight and ten
dollars a day, the workmen will not come at all: they will merely
send their cards.

I do not see any possible fault in the above figures. I ought to
say that I deferred putting a value on the potatoes until I had
footed up the debit column. This is always the safest way to do. I
had twenty-five bushels. I roughly estimated that there are one
hundred good ones to the bushel. Making my own market-price,
I asked two cents apiece for them. This I should have considered
dirt cheap last June, when I was going down the rows with the
hoe. If any one thinks that two cents each is high, let him try to
raise them.

Nature is "awful smart." I intend to be complimentary in saying so. She shows it in little things. I have mentioned my attempt
to put in a few modest turnips, near the close of the season. I
sowed the seeds, by the way, in the most liberal manner. Into
three or four short rows I presume I put enough to sow an acre;
and they all came up,---came up as thick as grass, as crowded and
useless as babies in a Chinese village. Of course, they had to be
thinned out; that is, pretty much all pulled up; and it took me a
long time; for it takes a conscientious man some time to decide
which are the best and healthiest plants to spare. After all, I

too many. That is the great danger everywhere in this
world (it may not be in the next); things are too thick: we lose all
in grasping for too much. The Scotch say, that no man ought to
thin out his own turnips, because he will not sacrifice enough to
leave room for the remainder to grow: he should get his neighbor, who does not care for the plants, to do it. But this is mere
talk, and aside from the point: if there is any thing I desire to
avoid in these agricultural papers, it is digression. I did think,
that putting in these turnips so late in the season, when general
activity has ceased, and in a remote part of the garden, they
would pass unnoticed. But Nature never even winks, as I can see.
The tender blades were scarcely out of the ground, when she
sent a small black fly, which seemed to have been born and held
in reserve for this purpose,—to cut the leaves. They speedily
made lace-work of the whole bed. Thus every thing appears to
have its special enemy,—except, perhaps, p——y: nothing ever
troubles that.

Did the Concord Grape ever come to more luscious perfection than this year? or yield so abundantly? The golden sunshine
has passed into them, and distended their purple skins almost to
bursting. Such heavy clusters! such bloom! such sweetness! such
meat and drink in their round globes! What a fine fellow Bacchus
would have been, if he had only signed the pledge when he was
a young man! I have taken off clusters that were as compact and
almost as large as the Black Hamburgs. It is slow work picking
them. I do not see how the gatherers for the vintage ever get off
enough. It takes so long to disentangle the bunches from the
leaves, and the interlacing vines, and the supporting tendrils;
and then I like to hold up each bunch and look at it in the sunlight, and get the fragrance and the bloom of it, and show it to
Polly, who is making herself useful, as taster and companion, at

the foot of the ladder, before dropping it into the basket. have other company. The robin, the most knowing and gr bird out of paradise (I trust he will always be kept out), has d covered that the grape-crop is uncommonly good, and has come back, with his whole tribe and family, larger than it was in pea-time. He knows the ripest bunches as well as anybody, and tries them all. If he would take a whole bunch here and there, say half the number, and be off with it, I should not so much care. But he will not. He pecks away at all the bunches, and spoils as many as he can. It is time he went south.

There is no prettier sight, to my eye, than a gardener on a ladder in his grape-arbor, in these golden days, selecting the heaviest clusters of grapes, and handing them down to one and another of a group of neighbors and friends, who stand under the shade of the leaves, flecked with the sunlight, and cry, "How sweet!" "What nice ones!" and the like,—remarks encouraging to the man on the ladder. It is great pleasure to see people eat grapes.

Moral Truth.—I have no doubt that grapes taste best in other peoples' mouths. It is an old notion that it is easier to be generous than to be stingy. I am convinced that the majority of people would be generous from selfish motives, if they had the opportunity.

Philosophical Observation.—Nothing shows one who his friends are, like prosperity and ripe fruit. I had a good friend in the country, whom I almost never visited except in cherry-time. By your fruits you shall know them.

SEVENTEENTH WEEK

I like to go into the garden these warm latter days, and muse. To muse is to sit in the sun, and not think of any thing. I am not sure but goodness comes out of people who bask in the sun, as it does out of a sweet apple roasted before the fire. The late September and October sun of this latitude is something like the sun of extreme Lower Italy: you can stand a good deal of it, and apparently soak a winter supply into the system. If one only could take in his winter fuel in this way! The next great discovery will, very likely, be the conservation of sunlight. In the correlation of forces, I look to see the day when the superfluous sunshine will be utilized; as, for instance, that which has burned up my celery this year will be converted into a force to work the garden.

This sitting in the sun amid the evidences of a ripe year is the easiest part of gardening I have experienced. But what a combat has gone on here! What vegetable passions have run the whole

gamut of ambition, selfishness, greed of place, fruition
and now rest here in the truce of exhaustion! What a battle
if one may look upon it so! The corn has lost its ammunition, a
stacked arms in a slovenly, militia sort of style. The ground vines
are torn, trampled, and withered; and the ungathered cucumbers, worthless melons, and golden squashes, lie about like the
spent bombs and exploded shells of a battle-field. So the can-
nonballs lay on the sandy plain before Fort Fisher, after the capture. So the great, grassy meadow at Munich, any morning
during the October Fest, is strewn with the empty beer-mugs.
History constantly repeats itself. There is a large crop of moral
reflections in my garden, which anybody is at liberty to gather
who passes this way.

I have tried to get in any thing that offered temptation to sin.
There would be no thieves if there was nothing to steal; and I
suppose, in the thieves' catechism, the provider is as bad as the
thief; and, probably, I am to blame for leaving out a few winter-
pears, which some predatory boy carried off on Sunday. At first,
I was angry, and said I should like to have caught the urchin in
the act; but, on second thought, I was glad I did not. The interview could not have been pleasant. I shouldn't have known what
to do with him. The chances are, that he would have escaped
away with his pockets full, and jibed at me from a safe distance.
And, if I had got my hands on him, I should have been still more
embarrassed. If I had flogged him, he would have got over it a
good deal sooner than I should. That sort of boy does not mind
castigation any more than he does tearing his trousers in the
briers. If I had treated him with kindness, and conciliated him
with grapes, showing him the enormity of his offence, I suppose
he would have come the next night, and taken the remainder of

es. The truth is, that the public morality is lax on the
t of fruit. If anybody puts arsenic or gunpowder into his
ermelons, he is universally denounced as a stingy old mur-
derer by the community. A great many people regard growing
fruit as lawful prey, who would not think of breaking into your
cellar to take it. I found a man once in my raspberry-bushes,
early in the season, when we were waiting for a dish-full to ripen.
Upon inquiring what he was about, he said he was only eating
some; and the operation seemed to be so natural and simple, that
I disliked to disturb him. And I am not very sure that one has a
right to the whole of an abundant crop of fruit until he has gathered it. At least, in a city garden, one might as well conform his
theory to the practice of the community.

As for children (and it sometimes looks as if the chief prod-
ucts of my garden were small boys and hens), it is admitted that
they are barbarians. There is no exception among them to this
condition of barbarism. This is not to say that they are not attractive; for they have the virtues as well as the vices of a primi-
tive people. It is held by some naturalists, that the child is only a
zoöphyte, with a stomach, and feelers radiating from it in search
of something to fill it. It is true that a child is always hungry all
over: but he is also curious all over; and his curiosity is excited
about as early as his hunger. He immediately begins to put out
his moral feelers into the unknown and the infinite to discover
what sort of an existence this is into which he has come. His
imagination is quite as hungry as his stomach. And again and
again it is stronger than his other appetites. You can easily engage his imagination in a story which will make him forget his
dinner. He is credulous and superstitious, and open to all wonder. In this, he is exactly like the savage races. Both gorge them-

selves on the marvellous; and all the unknown is marvel
them. I know the general impression is, that children mu.
governed through their stomachs. I think they can be controll
quite as well through their curiosity; that being the more craving
and imperious of the two. I have seen children follow about a
person who told them stories, and interested them with his
charming talk, as greedily as if his pockets had been full of *bon-bons.*

Perhaps this fact has no practical relation to gardening; but it
occurs to me, that, if I should paper the outside of my high
board fence with the leaves of "The Arabian Nights," it would
afford me a good deal of protection,—more, in fact, than spikes
in the top, which tear trousers, and encourage profanity, but do
not save much fruit. A spiked fence is a challenge to any boy of
spirit. But, if the fence were papered with fairy-tales, would he
not stop to read them until it was too late for him to climb into
the garden? I don't know. Human nature is vicious. The boy
might regard the picture of the garden of the Hesperides only as
an advertisement of what was over the fence. I begin to find that
the problem of raising fruit is nothing to that of getting it after it
has matured. So long as the law, just in many respects, is in force
against shooting birds and small boys, the gardener may sow in
tears and reap in vain.

The power of a boy is, to me, something fearful. Consider
what he can do. You buy and set out a choice pear-tree; you en-
rich the earth for it; you train and trim it, and vanquish the borer,
and watch its slow growth. At length it rewards your care by pro-
ducing two or three pears, which you cut up and divide in the
family, declaring the flavor of the bit you eat to be something ex-
traordinary. The next year, the little tree blossoms full, and sets

d in the autumn has on its slender, drooping limbs half a
el of fruit, daily growing more delicious in the sun. You
ow it to your friends, reading to them the French name, which
you can never remember, on the label; and you take an honest
pride in the successful fruit of long care. That night your pears
shall be required of you by a boy! Along comes an irresponsible
urchin, who has not been growing much longer than the tree,
with not twenty-five cents' worth of clothing on him, and in five
minutes takes off every pear, and retires into safe obscurity. In
five minutes, the remorseless boy has undone your work of
years, and with the easy *nonchalance,* I doubt not, of any agent of
fate, in whose path nothing is sacred or safe.

And it is not of much consequence. The boy goes on his
way,—to Congress, or to State Prison: in either place he will be
accused of stealing, perhaps wrongfully. You learn, in time, that
it is better to have had pears and lost them, than not to have had
pears at all. You come to know that the least (and rarest) part of
the pleasure of raising fruit is the vulgar eating it. You recall
your delight in conversing with the nurseryman, and looking at
his illustrated catalogues, where all the pears are drawn perfect
in form, and of extra size, and at that exact moment between
ripeness and decay which it is so impossible to hit in practice.
Fruit cannot be raised on this earth to taste as you imagine those
pears would taste. For years you have this pleasure, unalloyed by
any disenchanting reality. How you watch the tender twigs in
spring, and the freshly-forming bark, hovering about the healthy
growing tree with your pruning-knife many a sunny morning!
That is happiness. Then, if you know it, you are drinking the
very wine of life; and when the sweet juices of the earth mount
the limbs, and flow down the tender stem, ripening and redden-
ing the pendent fruit, you feel that you somehow stand at the

source of things, and have no unimportant share in the p
of Nature. Enter, at this moment, boy the destroyer, whose
is that of preserver as well; for, though he removes the fruit fr
your sight, it remains in your memory immortally ripe and de-
sirable. The gardener needs all these consolations of a high philosophy.

EIGHTEENTH WEEK

Regrets are idle; yet history is one long regret. Every thing might have turned out so differently! If Ravaillac had not been imprisoned for debt, he would not have stabbed Henry of Navarre. If William of Orange had escaped assassination by Philip's emissaries; if France had followed the French Calvin, and embraced Protestant Calvinism, as it came very near doing towards the end of the sixteenth century; if the Continental ammunition had not given out at Bunker's Hill; if Blucher had not "come up" at Waterloo—the lesson is, that things do not come up unless they are planted. When you go behind the historical scenery, you find there is a rope and pulley to effect every transformation which has astonished you. It was the rascality of a minister and a contractor five years before that lost the battle; and the cause of the defeat was worthless ammunition. I should like to know how many wars have been caused by fits of indigestion, and how many more dynasties have been upset by the love of woman

than by the hate of man. It is only because we are ill in
that any thing surprises us; and we are disappointed becau.
expect that for which we have not provided.

I had too vague expectations of what my garden would do of
itself. A garden ought to produce one every thing,—just as a
business ought to support a man, and a house ought to keep itself. We had a convention lately to resolve that the house should
keep itself; but it won't. There has been a lively time in our garden this summer; but it seems to me there is very little to show
for it. It has been a terrible campaign; but where is the indem-
nity? Where are all "sass" and Lorraine? It is true that we have
lived on the country; but we desire, besides, the fruits of the war.
There are no onions, for one thing. I am quite ashamed to take
people into my garden, and have them notice the absence of
onions. It is very marked. An onion is strength; and a garden without it lacks flavor. The onion in its satin wrappings is among the
most beautiful of vegetables; and it is the only one that repre-
sents the essence of things. It can almost be said to have a soul.
You take off coat after coat, and the onion is still there; and,
when the last one is removed, who dare say that the onion itself
is destroyed, though you can weep over its departed spirit? If
there is any one thing on this fallen earth that the angels in
heaven weep over more than another, it is the onion.

I know that there is supposed to be a prejudice against the
onion; but I think there is rather a cowardice in regard to it. I
doubt not that all men and women love the onion; but few confess
their love. Affection for it is concealed. Good New-Englanders
are as shy of owning it as they are of talking about religion.
Some people have days on which they eat onions,—what you
might call "retreats," or their "Thursdays." The act is in the nature of a religious ceremony, an Eleusinian mystery: not a breath

st get abroad. On that day, they see no company; they
the kiss of greeting to the dearest friend; they retire within
mselves, and hold communion with one of the most pungent
and penetrating manifestations of the moral vegetable world.
Happy is said to be the family which can eat onions together.
They are, for the time being, separate from the world, and have
a harmony of aspiration. There is a hint here for the reformers.
Let them become apostles of the onion; let them eat, and preach
it to their fellows, and circulate tracts of it in the form of seeds.
In the onion is the hope of universal brotherhood. If all men will
eat onions at all times, they will come into a universal sympathy.
Look at Italy. I hope I am not mistaken as to the cause of her
unity. It was the Reds who preached the gospel which made it
possible. All the Reds of Europe, all the sworn devotees of the
mystic Mary Ann, eat of the common vegetable. Their oaths
are strong with it. It is the food, also, of the common people of
Italy. All the social atmosphere of that delicious land is laden
with it. Its odor is a practical democracy. In the churches all
are alike: there is one faith, one smell. The entrance of Victor
Emanuel into Rome is only the pompous proclamation of a
unity which garlic had already accomplished; and yet we, who
boast of our democracy, eat onions in secret.

I now see that I have left out many of the most moral ele-
ments. Neither onions, parsnips, carrots, nor cabbages are here. I
have never seen a garden in the autumn before, without the uncouth cabbage in it; but my garden gives the impression of a garden without a head. The cabbage is the rose of Holland. I admire
the force by which it compacts its crisp leaves into a solid head.
The secret of it would be priceless to the world. We should see
less expansive foreheads with nothing within. Even the largest
cabbages are not always the best. But I mention these things, not

from any sympathy I have with the vegetables named to show how hard it is to go contrary to the expectations of Society expects every man to have certain things in his gar. Not to raise cabbage is as if one had no pew in church. Perhaps we shall come some day to free churches and free gardens; when I can show my neighbor through my tired garden, at the end of the season, when skies are overcast, and brown leaves are swirling down, and not mind if he does raise his eyebrows when he observes, "Ah! I see you have none of this, and of that." At present, we want the moral courage to plant only what we need; to spend only what will bring us peace, regardless of what is going on over the fence. We are half ruined by conformity; but we should be wholly ruined without it: and I presume I shall make a garden next year that will be as popular as possible.

And this brings me to what I see may be a crisis in life. I begin to feel the temptation of experiment. Agriculture, horticulture, floriculture,—these are vast fields, into which one may wander away, and never be seen more. It seemed to me a very simple thing, this gardening; but it opens up astonishingly. It is like the infinite possibilities in worsted-work. Polly sometimes says to me, "I wish you would call at Bobbin's, and match that skein of worsted for me when you are in town." Time was I used to accept such a commission with alacrity and self-confidence. I went to Bobbin's, and asked one of his young men, with easy indifference, to give me some of *that*. The young man, who is as handsome a young man as ever I looked at, and who appears to own the shop, and whose suave superciliousness would be worth every thing to a cabinet minister who wanted to repel applicants for place, says, "I haven't an ounce: I have sent to Paris, and I expect it every day. I have a good deal of difficulty in getting that shade in my assortment." To think that he is in communication

, and perhaps with Persia! Respect for such a being ace to awe. I go to another shop, holding fast to my scar-ew. There I am shown a heap of stuff, with more colors and ades than I had supposed existed in all the world. What a blaze of distraction! I have been told to get as near the shade as I could; and so I compare and contrast, till the whole thing seems to me about of one color. But I can settle my mind on nothing. The affair assumes a high degree of importance. I am satisfied with nothing but perfection. I don't know what may happen if the shade is not matched. I go to another shop, and another, and another. At last a pretty girl, who could make any customer believe that green is blue, matches the shade in a minute. I buy five cents' worth. That was the order. Women are the most economical persons that ever were. I have spent two hours in this five-cent business; but who shall say they were wasted, when I take the stuff home, and Polly says it is a perfect match, and looks so pleased, and holds it up with the work, at arm's-length, and turns her head one side, and then takes her needle, and works it in? Working in, I can see, my own obligingness and amiability with every stitch. Five cents is dirt cheap for such a pleasure.

The things I may do in my garden multiply on my vision. How fascinating have the catalogues of the nurserymen become! Can I raise all those beautiful varieties, each one of which is preferable to the other? Shall I try all the kinds of grapes, and all the sorts of pears? I have already fifteen varieties of strawberries (vines); and I have no idea that I have hit the right one. Must I subscribe to all the magazines and weekly papers which offer premiums of the best vines? Oh that all the strawberries were rolled into one, that I could enclose all its lusciousness in one bite! Oh for the good old days when a strawberry was a strawberry, and there was no perplexity about it! There are more

berries now than churches; and no one knows wha[
have seen gardens which were all experiment, give[
every new thing, and which produced little or nothing
owners, except the pleasure of expectation. People grow pe
trees at great expense of time and money, which never yielα
them more than four pears to the tree. The fashions of ladies'
bonnets are nothing to the fashions of nurserymen. He who at-
tempts to follow them has a business for life; but his life may be
short. If I enter upon this wide field of horticultural experiment,
I shall leave peace behind; and I may expect the ground to open,
and swallow me and all my fortune. May Heaven keep me to the
old roots and herbs of my forefathers! Perhaps, in the world of
modern reforms, this is not possible; but I intend now to cultivate only the standard things, and learn to talk knowingly of the
rest. Of course, one must keep up a reputation. I have seen people greatly enjoy themselves, and elevate themselves in their
own esteem, in a wise and critical talk about all the choice wines,
while they were sipping a decoction, the original cost of which
bore no relation to the price of grapes.

NINETEENTH WEEK

The closing scenes are not necessarily funereal. A garden should be got ready for winter as well as for summer. When one goes into winter-quarters, he wants every thing neat and trim. Expecting high winds, we bring every thing into close reef. Some men there are who never shave (if they are so absurd as ever to shave), except when they go abroad, and who do not take care to wear polished boots in the bosoms of their families. I like a man who shaves (next to one who doesn't shave) to satisfy his own conscience, and not for display, and who dresses as neatly at home as he does anywhere. Such a man will be likely to put his garden in complete order before the snow comes, so that its last days shall not present a scene of melancholy ruin and decay.

I confess, that, after such an exhausting campaign, I felt a great temptation to retire, and call it a drawn engagement. But better counsels prevailed. I determined that the weeds should not sleep on the field of battle. I routed them out, and levelled

their works. I am master of the situation. If I have ma
I at least have peace; but it is not quite a desert. The stra
the raspberries, the celery, the turnips, wave green abo
clean earth, with no enemy in sight. In these golden Octo
days, no work is more fascinating than this getting ready for
spring. The sun is no longer a burning enemy, but a friend, illu-
minating all the open space, and warming the mellow soil. And
the pruning and clearing-away of rubbish, and the fertilizing, go
on with something of the hilarity of a wake, rather than the de-
spondency of other funerals. When the wind begins to come out
of the north-west of set purpose, and to sweep the ground with
low and searching fierceness, very different from the roystering,
jolly bluster of early fall, I have put the strawberries under their
coverlet of leaves, pruned the grape-vines and laid them under
the soil, tied up the tender plants, given the fruit-trees a good,
solid meal about the roots, and so I turn away, writing *Resurgam*
on the gate-post. And Calvin, aware that the summer is past and
the harvest is ended, and that a mouse in the kitchen is worth
two birds gone south, scampers away to the house with his tail in
the air.

And yet I am not perfectly at rest in my mind. I know that this
is only a truce until the parties recover their exhausted energies.
All winter long, the forces of chemistry will be mustering under
ground, repairing the losses, calling up the reserves, getting new
strength from my surface-fertilizing bounty, and making ready
for the spring campaign. They will open it before I am ready:
while the snow is scarcely melted, and the ground is not pass-
able, they will begin to move on my works; and the fight will
commence. Yet how deceitfully it will open to the music of birds
and the soft enchantment of the spring mornings! I shall even be
permitted to win a few skirmishes: the secret forces will even

.o plant and sow, and show my full hand, before they
in heavy and determined assault. There are already
of an internecine fight with the devil-grass, which has in-
nched itself in a considerable portion of my garden-patch. It
contests the ground inch by inch; and digging it out is very much
such labor as eating a piece of choke-cherry-pie with the stones
all in. It is work, too, that I know by experience I shall have to
do alone. Every man must eradicate his own devil-grass. The
neighbors who have leisure to help you in grape-picking time
are all busy when devil-grass is most aggressive. My neighbors'
visits are well timed: it is only their hens which have all seasons
for their own.

I am told that abundant and rank weeds are signs of a rich
soil; but I have noticed that a thin, poor soil grows little but
weeds. I am inclined to think that the substratum is the same,
and that the only choice in this world is what kind of weeds you
will have. I am not much attracted by the gaunt, flavorless mul-
lein, and the wiry thistle of upland country pastures, where the
grass is always gray, as if the world were already weary and sick
of life. The awkward, uncouth wickedness of remote country-
places, where culture has died out after the first crop, is about as
disagreeable as the ranker and richer vice of city life, forced by
artificial heat and the juices of an overfed civilization. There is
no doubt, that, on the whole, the rich soil is the best: the fruit of
it has body and flavor. To what affluence does a woman (to take
an instance, thank Heaven, which is common) grow, with favor-
ing circumstances, under the stimulus of the richest social and
intellectual influences! I am aware that there has been a good
deal said in poetry about the fringed gentian and the harebell of
rocky districts and waysides, and I know that it is possible for
maidens to bloom in very slight soil into a wild-wood grace and

beauty; yet, the world through, they lack that we
that tropic affluence of both person and mind, whic.
more stimulating culture brings:—the passion as well as
glowing in the Cloth-of-Gold rose. Neither persons nor p
are ever fully themselves until they are cultivated to their hig.
est. I, for one, have no fear that society will be too much en-
riched. The only question is about keeping down the weeds; and
I have learned by experience, that we need new sorts of hoes,
and more disposition to use them.

Moral Deduction.—The difference between soil and society is
evident. We bury decay in the earth; we plant in it the perishing;
we feed it with offensive refuse: but nothing grows out of it that
is not clean; it gives us back life and beauty for our rubbish. Society returns us what we give it.

Pretending to reflect upon these things, but, in reality, watching the blue-jays, who are pecking at the purple berries of the
woodbine on the south gable, I approach the house. Polly is
picking up chestnuts on the sward, regardless of the high wind,
which rattles them about her head and upon the glass roof of her
winter-garden. The garden, I see, is filled with thrifty plants,
which will make it always summer there. The callas about the
fountain will be in flower by Christmas: the plant appears to
keep that holiday in her secret heart all summer. I close the outer
windows as we go along, and congratulate myself that we are
ready for winter. For the winter-garden I have no responsibility: Polly has entire charge of it. I am only required to keep it
heated, and not too hot either; to smoke it often for the death of
the bugs; to water it once a day; to move this and that into the
sun and out of the sun pretty constantly: but she does all the
work. We never relinquish that theory.

As we pass around the house, I discover a boy in the ravine, chestnuts and hickory-nuts. They are not plenty

I suggest the propriety of leaving some for us. The

little slow to take the idea: but he has apparently found

cking poor, and exhausted it; for, as he turns away down the

en, he hails me with,—

"Mister, I say, can you tell me where I can find some walnuts?"

The coolness of this world grows upon me. It is time to go in and light a wood-fire on the hearth.

About the Author

Charles Dudley Warner was born in 1829. He received a law degree from the University of Pennsylvania and then practiced law in Chicago before moving to Connecticut, where he became an associate editor and publisher of *The Hartford Courant*. In addition to writing travel essays for the *Courant* and *Harper's* magazine, as well as several novels, he also collaborated with his close friend Mark Twain on *The Gilded Age*. He died in 1900.